One Pedal at a Time

A Novice Caregiver and Her Cyclist Husband Face Their New Normal with Courage, Tenacity and Abundant Love.

CJ Golden

*To June +
Laurie +
Julia's Round Trip —*

*May you
overcome all your
"hills" one Pedal
at a time :
Love
Bob + Becky*

ERONEL
PUBLISHING

Published by Eronel Publishing, Plymouth, VT.

Library of Congress Cataloguing in Publication Data
Golden CJ
One Pedal at a Time by CJ Golden
Biography & Autobiography: Personal Memoir | Body, Mind & Spirit | Family & Relationships
Library of Congress Control Number: 2018931791

Eronel Publishing
2018

First Edition

Cover photo by Creed McPherson

Also by CJ Golden

TAO OF THE DEFIANT WOMAN
Five Brazen Ways to Accept What You Must
and Rebel Against the Rest

TAO-GIRLS RULE!
Finding Balance, Staying Confident,
Being Bold in a World of Challenges

**For Alix, Emily, Josh,
Benjamin and Harrison**

May you always know how brave your Boopah is.

And to Joe

For teaching me about the power of courage
and the strength of love

Table of Contents

Prologue

His cane with three feet
Moving with care
Holding my hand as we walk cross the street
Me in my leg brace
Mirror image of his
We laugh about running a three-legged race

Young onlookers grin
At this couple so aged
They don't quite believe we are not at all dim

We have become *that* couple
That couple one finds
And thinks of as frail
Yes, maybe of body but not in our minds
In the past we would see
Others looking disabled
Back before we were the new he and me
We would try to not stare
Feeling so smug
We still had our strength but knew life is not fair
But we now are *that* couple
That couple one finds
And feels sorry for
But we now understand frail is all in one's mind
We do what we must
Caregivers and takers
Understanding our love deepens with trust

Laugh with our friends
Meet them for dinner
A cane and a brace doesn't mean our life ends
Yet we are *that* couple

And it is our duty
To remain strong of soul
For *that* couple's life still holds so much beauty
We are not close to finished
The world needs to know this
We're dynamic, alert, spirit never diminished

We still share a love
That transcends any weakness
In heart we are strong and thank Heaven above
That we are *this* couple.

~ CJ Golden

INTRODUCTION

"From caring comes courage."
~Lao Tzu

I sat in stunned disbelief as I heard the words, assaulting and cruel, as if passed down by a punitive judge. "We are releasing him from the hospital next week. There is no more we can do for him here; medically he is stable. We suggest you find another placement – a step-down facility. You cannot care for him at home."

My mind reeled and my senses went into overdrive as I tried, in vain, to get an extension of at least a week.

The leukemia cells that had invaded his central nervous system – mimicking the symptoms of stroke – had rendered Joe completely, physically helpless. Yet, surely in a week, I hoped, with illogical optimism, Joe would be weaned off his feeding tube. Certainly, in the span of seven more days he would no longer need the catheter. And, most important of all, the extension of time would find him stronger; capable of transferring from his hospital bed to a wheelchair without the need of the huge machine that grabbed him, much like a fork-lift, and moved his body from one spot to another.

But, the head of the rehabilitation unit was relentless and unmoving. Joe was to be discharged and there was no debating this decision.

I did not listen to them and send him to a sub-acute facility. Against all their pressing, I chose to bring him home.

What I did not know at the time of that infamous meeting was that Dr. Schmidt was correct. An extra week in the hospital would not have made a difference. By the second week home, Joe was still hooked up to his catheter and feeding tube, still required the ridiculously, heavy machine to move him, and, while medically becoming more stable, he was still greatly physically incapacitated.

I was totally unprepared for the job of being his caregiver. I'd done it earlier the same year; that was the stroke that hospitalized him for five weeks. But, he had bounced back quickly and almost completely by the time he'd been released. My duties then as caregiver were just about nil.

This was different; so very different. And, this time I had to call upon all the resources I could muster – physically, emotionally, mentally, spiritually and financially. We were fortunate, Joe and I, to have the financial means with which to hire a private-duty nurse to help. And, we were able to arrange for the special equipment that Medicare did not cover. I will never take that for granted, and I recognize the ability to cover these special costs removed a great burden off our shoulders. *I also recognize that many others do not share these same financial advantages and, therefore, have included a resource section at the end of this book that, hopefully, will help you find the aid you need and deserve – caregivers' support groups, financial assistance agencies and other valuable and appropriate resources.*

Dispensing my duties as Joe's primary caregiver, nurse, "mother," my mind kept going to the adage that what doesn't kill you makes you stronger.

I was not sure which was going to strike first.

PART ONE:

For Better or For Worse

Chapter One:
Love Renewed

Within a year after the divorce from my first husband, I was most certainly not on the prowl for another man in my life. Yet one day, as I arrived from the bus that had brought me back home from a job interview in New York City, I walked into the office of our travel agent, Joe Golden.

My ex and I had known Joe for many years as a member of our small community in Danbury, Connecticut. We'd seen each other from time to time and, when Joe had been married, there were some events that included him and his wife, along with my then-husband and several other couples of the same age and stage in life.

Joe was always ready and willing to help us with whatever travel information we required for our various vacations and business trips. He was good. He was kind. And, he was very pleasant to speak to.

So, when I went to Joe's office to have him arrange travel for me to go to Florida and visit my parents (this predated our being able to boot-up our computers and make these arrangements ourselves) it was not a surprise to me that I was supremely comfortable in his presence.

Now, here's a bit of an admission I had not previously shared with many, I walked out of Joe's office a bit tipsy – not on drink or meds – but with an unusual feeling that told me this man was going to be an important part of my life one day. It was, to say the least, weird, a little scary, but greatly exhilarating and exciting.

Our friendship grew slowly, carefully, with Joe very attuned to the fact that I was recently divorced and not ready to begin a new relationship as he was, having been divorced for five years.

He was patient and caring. I never felt pushed. What I did feel was loved and liked and respected.

Truth be told, when Joe was interviewed for this book, he was asked what it was that had attracted him to me. He responded that he "was looking for someone, timing was perfect. Knew Caryn for years when we were both married to others." And in his estimation the reason it worked, "She was happy-go-lucky, we laughed a lot, easy to talk to, just clicked."

Thanks, Joe!

Then, one auspicious evening, I was introduced to his mother who was visiting from her home in Florida. After our dinner together, while Joe was driving back to his house, her words clinched the deal, "She's a nice girl."

Following that was a visit to my folks who were also in Florida, a meeting of the parents and, as tradition dictates, we were now ready to openly proclaim our love and desire to get married. At that point, we'd been together for more than three years, and I knew it was time for me to move on, completely, with my life – and that included spending the rest of my days with Joe.

We told our children one evening when we were all in the car together going out to dinner. How wonderful that they were thrilled! Life could not have felt more perfect.

The wedding planners (that would be Joe and me and the kids) got to work.

And so, at our home on Sunday, May 26, 1991, on a perfectly gorgeous afternoon, our union was affirmed as I walked out of our house in my off-white wedding dress, hair up and wound around a headpiece of flowers, headed to my soon-to-be husband and my new life as Mrs. Joe Golden.

Joe was waiting for me, next to our Rabbi, in the swing arbor that had been purchased for this extraordinary day. The traditional wedding march was replaced by the touching rendition of "our" song - Aaron Neville's and Linda Ronstadt's "I Don't Know Much" – as my son's keyboard expertise accompanied his girlfriend's sweet singing.

Forty guests, including our parents, closest friends and family members cheered as the ceremony was concluded and we began our new life together.

The bar-b-que meal was spectacular but not nearly as much as our wedding cake – which sported, not only the names of the bride and groom, but all four of our children. This was not only a marriage of one man and one woman. This was the marriage of two families who, as we could have never understood at the time, were destined to become as strong and loving, supportive and caring as any family could ever be.

We were now not merely a wedded couple, but a growing family, growing in number and strength and the connections of love. And, becoming part of each other to form a bond that was preordained to become stronger through the years.

None of us could have imagined the test that was going to be thrown our way twenty-five years down the road.

Twenty-five years of marriage, usually a time of great celebration and one that Joe and I personally looked forward to, as neither of us had made it to a twenty-fifth anniversary our first times around. It was not the celebration we had anticipated.

Chapter Two:
Stronger Together

On one of our first dates, Joe took me for a hike at a local park. It was a relatively even and well-cut trail that did not require major hiking skills to navigate. That was fine with me as I was far from an experienced hiker.

He and I went hand in hand over the terrain taking in the beauty of a bright fall afternoon. Until we came upon a wall. Not a tall wall, but imposing nevertheless, and one that we were going to have to circumnavigate in order to continue on our way. That, however, was not going to happen, as it seemed to stretch for miles in either direction. The only way past it, it appeared, was to go over this seemingly unnavigable barrier.

"No way," I exclaimed. "I cannot climb over that wall." His rejoinder was not a sympathetic nod of understanding, but a shake of his head and a facial expression that told me he was going to accept nothing less than me overcoming my fear and getting from one side of the wall to the other. He didn't know that he was dealing with a first-class wimp; a woman who still pictured herself wearing her pretty little school dresses and patent leather shoes – clothing that would preclude wall climbing, or any other physical activity that required "tomboy" skills. Joe, on the other hand had always been daring, challenging the elements (along with, I am told, his teachers and parents). He'd been on the football team in school and a state championship wrestler. No way was he going to allow me to remain the timid little girl. Nope, he was going to do his darndest to exorcise that demon and help bring out the self-confident woman he knew was hiding deep within me.

Scrambling over the rocks and holding his hand out to help steady me, Joe managed to get me, not only over the wall, but also over my fear. His steady encouragement has helped me enjoy hiking in thirty-nine of our national parks together and taught me the joys of pitching a tent and camping out.

Joe has been my rock as I have learned to grow secure in my abilities – whether they are in my various careers, tackling extracurricular activities (Banjo lessons for a fifty-year old? Not absurd with Joe urging me on), growing comfortable in my own skin and even accepting my birthdays with grace and good humor.

I, on the other hand, have managed to help this man who would appear to be all-wise in matters that had stymied him – relating to a seventeen-year-old daughter being one of those. It has been my joy to encourage him as he started his own business, or trained for marathon bike rides.

Together we learned to appreciate each other's love of sports (his), country music (mine), theater (me again) and dancing. Okay, he never did get into dancing – but I sure did try.

We were a team when it came to caring for our aging and ailing parents, loving our four children and five grandkids, spending time with close friends, and relaxing on our own – enjoying the company we provide for each other.

Our love, mutual respect and friendship continue to grow in strength and intensity as the years fly by.

Anything we had borne together, was nothing compared to Joe having to become nurse to me after I had my first of three back surgeries.

In 2007, it was discovered that the immense pain radiating down my right leg was emanating from my back; "spinal stenosis" said the orthopedic surgeon and, after a series of injections that did not relieve my pain, it was deemed that surgery was the only option.

A one-night stay in the hospital after surgery turned into two, but once home, I quickly recovered, and Joe's nursing duties were not major. Then, two years later came back surgery number two and, that having been done as an outpatient, left me tired and a bit wobbly, but capable of handling the task of hosting our family Thanksgiving dinner just ten days later.

It was the hand surgery that created more of a problem. The post-surgical pain was immense, and Joe was forced to watch me cry in fits of agony for many weeks until all began to settle down. Thereafter, he was called upon (often) to offer his services when I tried to complete a two-handed task with just one. He became, literally, my right hand. Well, he had been since the beginning of our relationship so why not now? Once again, Joe rose to the challenge and was supremely capable and caring.

September 2014 saw my third – and most extensive – back surgery. While it was successful in eliminating the pain caused by scoliosis, it created a new problem having damaged the peroneal nerve that runs down from one's spine to the foot, thus causing what is so charmingly called "drop foot."

That was a doozy and the greatest challenge for us to deal with to that point in time. The pain I experienced was immense even after three weeks in the hospital on IV pain medication. By the time I came home, I was a wreck, but Joe – nurse extraordinaire that he was – came to my rescue with in-bed coffee service, extra hands to help me move gingerly from room to room and pushing me to take that much needed afternoon nap, cuddling the little get-well bear Joe had given to me when I had awoken from the surgery. He fielded phone calls, ushered in caring friends when they visited and helped me with personal hygiene.

Thus began a journey that brought me from fear to determination as I learned to walk with my brace. First with walker. Next with cane. And finally, unaided.

Joe's presence and calm demeanor gave me a sense of peace. When I burrowed under the covers and felt him next to me at night I felt safe. When he appeared in the morning with my cup of coffee and amply buttered toast, I felt nourished in body and soul. When he gently laced my slippers on my feet and helped me get dressed for the day I felt loved.

There was something about my situation and lack of mobility that brought me back to my childhood. I needed the physical and emotional help that Joe was providing. He became my mentor and caregiver – just as my parents had been when I was a child.

And, he kept me sheltered from the unknown forces that might be waiting in the Universe to harm me. I had no idea what those might be, but in times of personal frailty one feels subject to unknown dangers, especially after having suffered a sudden trauma. Might it happen again? With Joe at my side, I felt more at peace with the thought that I was – and would stay - on the path of healing. He would hold the demons at bay.

I do remember the morning, however, when he arrived at my bedside with my coffee and breakfast and announced that was the last day of such service. I was to get myself up and out of bed the next morning as the days of lounging and luxury were over.

How mean. How insightful. How right.

He knew just when the time had come for me to begin pushing myself a tad more, and I balked outwardly as I nodded in agreement within.

We'd been through the mill together, survived all the emergencies – small and large – and each time came through stronger and more in love than before.

Yet, I did tell Joe – in no uncertain terms – that he had better not ever get sick for there was no way I would be strong enough, capable enough, or emotionally stable enough to be a caregiver to him as he had been to me through all my ailments.

Now, the tables have turned, and it is Joe who has been incapacitated, and I have, suddenly, and with great trepidation, assumed the role of caregiver.

As I helped him with his morning routine of getting out of bed into his wheelchair or walker, going into the bathroom to wash, brush his teeth and get dressed, then making his way into the kitchen where I toast his English muffin, pour his orange juice and ready his pills, I wonder if he felt as I did when he watched over me.

I hope he does.

I hope that Joe feels safe in my care and that he knows I will keep him from danger as best as I can.

That is what people do for each other in a loving relationship, for the marriage vow states, "in sickness and in health." We've had both and we keep getting stronger. And, together, we feel safe.

Chapter Three:
You Are a Writer

I've been fortunate through my life to have had – and enjoyed – several careers, which included being a speech therapist in our local schools back in the days when bringing such programs to the public school setting was quite innovative. After leaving the school system, I opened a private therapy clinic with a friend and colleague who was a reading specialist.

It was enormously rewarding for me to be able to help others through their own struggles, be it a child with a speech or language disorder or an adult who had suffered a debilitating illness – such as a stroke – and needed my help to relearn his or her communication skills.

Eventually, the acting bug that had first struck in college resurfaced and I began my life as a stage and screen actor. How much fun it was to be able to elicit emotions from an audience through a writer's words. I discovered I was rather adept at doing so and quickly went from local theatre to New York City and several soap operas and, finally, found my way under the big Hollywood sign.

During this stage of my life, I began to find the confidence I had always lacked, although, being an actor, I believe, I did a rather fine job of portraying a woman who was self-assured. But, putting myself out in the public eye, going through the rejections (there were so many) of casting directors at auditions, getting a couple of jobs and even finding the courage to join a small improvisation group in Hollywood, began to create in me a true sense of self. I did, indeed, have the talent to call myself an actor – albeit in only small roles – and it felt liberating.

Slowly, Caryn was morphing into CJ (my stage name) and becoming a truly self-assured person.

But, the job that has given me the most significant sense of self began the day that Joe read a rather pointed letter that I had written to a former friend.

After ingesting the words and the way in which I managed to get my point across, Joe looked at me and proclaimed, "You're a writer. You should write."

Just that. That mandate was so meaningful to me that I immediately signed up for a writing course at a local University, followed by another. And, my career as a writer was off and running.

Starting with short articles and poems that were submitted to, and published by, independent magazines and journals, I found that sitting at my computer, pulling the reflections ruminating in my head - and then being able to articulate them through the written word - helped to clarify my feelings,

The one thing I had not yet come to terms with was the idea of growing older. Of course, one wants to continue doing so, but each personal birthday was greeted with trepidation (how am I supposed to behave now that I am a year older?) and anger (looking older was rather annoying, to say the least.)

While visiting a friend, who was clearly elated that it was her birthday, I asked how she does it. "How do you celebrate getting older? Doesn't it bother you that the years are piling up?"

Her response was for me to speak to other women and get their input. What is it about getting older that they enjoy? What is it that hangs them up? "And then," she continued, "write a book about what you've learned. You're a writer. You should write."

There it was again. "You're a writer. You should write."

And, that was the birth of my first book. Combining the wisdom and acceptance of the ancient Chinese philosophy of Taoism with a touch of defiance (defying negativity and self-defeating behaviors), I targeted women who, like myself, continued to grow older (lucky us) but did not quite know how to do so joyfully.

That book spurred a similar work for teen and pre-teen girls and, those two, in turn, started my next career as public speaker and workshop facilitator. I had become a motivator to women and girls, and, in the process, finally came to like and respect myself.

I could not have imagined how my writing would help me through the most trying of situations when Joe became ill and I took over as his caregiver. Communicating through the written word – via email correspondence with family and friends, as I reported on his daily conditions, and blogs that helped to reinforce the lessons I was learning – got me through the trials of this last year. And, I discovered, helped others facing similar situations.

Having published many blogs throughout my writing career, they now took on a significance as no others had done. As I worked and wrote my way through Joe's illness, I never expected my words would take on a life of their own as motivators for others as well. And, now, they have worked their way into this book.

When I first approached Joe to share that my readers had pressed me to write this book, he was enthusiastic – very much so. Even when it was suggested by my editor that the "book will expose your life," Joe's response was that if it could help someone, it is good. "I don't care for my sake, and I'm better now."

That permission and encouragement, by the way, includes some of the rather absurd things he'd done that are shared in the following pages. In his words "I told Caryn to write the book, she's a natural to write it. And, she should put in those anecdotes. They are funny, and they should be shared."

Thanks, Joe, for your never-ending encouragement.

It is my hope that as the reader follows the path of this journal he/she will find faith and courage to face a similar trial. For there is always hope and lessons to be learned along the way.

Chapter Four:
Fire, Floods and Raccoons

Now that I was ready to celebrate my birthdays, I had decided that for my sixtieth I would join my daughter in Phoenix and, together with one of my closest friends, I'd participate in the Susan G. Komen Three Day, Sixty Mile Walk.

Logging twenty miles a day on sore and calloused feet, while helping to raise money for this very worthy cause, was one of the most exhilarating things I'd ever done. So much so that my daughter and I did it again the following year.

We were so very proud of ourselves for having logged such great distances. Until Joe raised the bar and decided he was going to ride his bicycle across the country in celebration of his upcoming sixtieth birthday.

And so, in 2007, the year before his milestone birthday, Joe, began to train by riding his cycle around town – increasing his mileage, speed and stamina as he went. For the main event, I was to be the SAG (support vehicle); we would plot a route and ride 100 miles a day. In a month, he'd be done. Not even close to realistic!

But I remained steady and ready to help him achieve this lofty goal until one day he came home and, with an apologetic face, told me he found a group he could ride with but that meant I would not be his SAG and go along.

It is hard to hold back that kind of joy, but I did; expressed that I was pleased for him, didn't let him know how unbelievably relieved I was and even tried to arrange my facial expressions into some semblance of sad/regret/disappointment.

In May 20, 2009, Joe and I drove down to Yorktown, Virginia where he was to embark on his trek to Florence, Oregon, a distance of 4,000 miles. That would be considered a daunting task for most, and especially for Joe, who'd not cycled further than around our neighborhood prior to undertaking this trip.

One might assume that he was not ready to undertake such a ride. One would be right.

Joe learned as he cycled; he learned the perseverance needed to tackle the mountains, he learned how difficult it is to ride sixty miles or more every day; he learned the art of setting up a tent quickly in the rain; he learned to endure a very sore butt as he sat upon his saddle. But, he also learned that tenacity and inner strength goes a long way towards achieving a major goal like this.

And, he did it. From leaving Yorktown in the pouring rain, to arriving in Florence in beautiful sunshine, Joe pedaled every single inch of the way; not once getting off the bike to walk up a mountain. Three months later, I flew to Florence to witness him achieve that destination with his fellow cyclists. I grinned with great pride as he dipped his rear bicycle wheels into the ocean (when embarking on a cross country trip like this, the riders begin by dipping the front bike wheels in the ocean and end with the rear wheels in the ocean on the other shore.)

Other long-distance rides followed; in 2012, he rode the Pacific Crest Trail from the Mexican border to the Canadian border.

His last (so far) ride was another cross-country trek from San Diego to St. Augustine, FL. that began on September 14, 2015.

It was that ride that now carries more significance than I ever thought possible, for it has become the standard by which we equate Joe's subsequent recovery from his devastating illnesses of 2016.

As difficult as it is to ride one's two-wheeler for thousands of miles, it was the state of Texas that tried its darndest to stonewall the cyclists. One thousand miles – a third of the entire trip – was comprised of Texas' terrain, climate, weather and fauna. Every possible obstacle was thrown in their paths. And those thousand miles came close to succeeding in ending the trip but for the stamina, endurance and down-right stubbornness of Joe, my long-distance, cyclist husband.

He and the group rode through hailstorms, passed massive fires, endured torrential rain, were waylaid by the ensuing floods, cycled hundreds of miles without access to water – other than the bottles packed on their already overweight bikes - set up their tents and were plagued by raccoons and fire ants, all while dealing with the state's monstrous heat.

Yet he endured, and watching Joe ride into the final destination of St. Augustine, Florida was one of the most joyous experiences of my life.

Neither of us could have possibly imagined that a mere six months later Joe would be embroiled in another intense challenge; one that tried to take his life.

There was no intense fire, nor were there floods or raccoons.

There was, however, the stroke caused by leukemia cells attacking his central nervous system.

We referred to his time in the hospital as Texas; for as he made his way through that, he would now have to employ the same fortitude and strength of character to get through the new challenge.

PART TWO:

Our Courage is Tested

Chapter Five:
The Events Unfold

~May, June~

May 2015

On May 26, 2015, Joe and I had celebrated our 24th anniversary with much joy and great anticipation of the upcoming 25th. We'd both been married before but neither of us had achieved that milestone. It was exciting to contemplate, and we envisioned a low-key celebration with all of our kids and grandkids.

We did not envision that our 25th wedding anniversary merriment the following year - May 26, 2016 - would be darkened by the knowledge that there was something seriously wrong with Joe. None of us knew what that might have been, but his slurred speech gave hints of a possible stroke.

Well, that's not exactly true, for when Joe was later asked about this period of time, he confessed that he knew he was having a stroke when he recognized his speech was slurred at a dinner with friends just before our anniversary. After that dinner, he had asked me if I noticed anything different about his speech and, quite honestly, I did not.

He knew, however, what was happening while I remained in the dark. I thought I was smarter than that – guess not. Or, I was in deep denial.

Thus began a year fraught with doctor visits and tests, spinal taps and a brain biopsy. And fear. So much fear.

Now, as I look back on the informational emails I had shared in the following days with concerned family and friends, I can see the evidence building that ultimately led to the severity of Joe's illness. At the time, of course, it was all a great mystery. All I could do was report the day-to-day medical news flashes. I did so via group emails as contacting each caring individual was more than I had the time or energy to do.

May 31, 2016 8:57PM

To our wonderful and caring friends and family,

Two years ago, Joe was diagnosed with CLL - Chronic Lymphocytic Leukemia -a type of cancer in which the bone marrow makes too many lymphocytes (a type of white blood cell).

It was discovered through a routine blood test done by Dr. Ruxin, our primary care doc. Because the test showed a very high white blood count, Joe was sent to a local oncologist for further evaluation.

Another blood test confirmed what that doctor had suspected: Joe had CLL. I was not there to hear that, and poor Joe had to come home and share the news with me.

It wasn't a big deal then because it was asymptomatic. But the symptoms seem to be appearing now - fatigue, weakness. In his words, he first realized something was wrong when biking with our son and "couldn't make it up the hills I used to laugh at."

That's why he is undergoing the CT scan today - to further assess the degree to which he has the disease.

And his greatly slurred speech shows us that he has also suffered a stroke at some point recently.

As for the CLL, a course of action must be decided on - which will be either chemo infusions for six months, or a drug in pill form (every day forever).

Joe's local hematologist/oncologist Dr. Rella agreed that we should get a second opinion before beginning a course of chemo for the CLL and, so we are contacting Dana Farber Cancer Institute in Boston and will make an appointment with an oncologist there.

By the way – Dr. Rella is competent and comforting – so much so that I got a hug from him as we were leaving the office! Boy, did we find the right guy.

This all, on top of the joy of celebrating our anniversary, has been a very emotional time.

Is there a book in here???

Love you all
Caryn

June 14 – 22, 2015

We had been in Quebec City in June of 2015, and on the 20th celebrated my birthday with a tour of that magnificent city followed by a sumptuous dinner at The Chateaux Fontenac - which is as classy as the name suggests. What a superb place to have marked another year on the calendar. Far better than where I spent my birthday the following year, which of course, I could never have predicted.

That following year we were in Boston where Joe was a patient at Brigham and Women's Hospital, with his oncologist, Dr. Eric Jacobsen from Dana Farber, taking charge of his case. And, on the day of my birthday, he was undergoing a brain biopsy to discern the cause of the stroke that had taken away his ability to speak and think clearly along with his loss of mobility.

He does not remember that day nor the procedure, but recently looked at me – while reading this over my shoulder, and asked bluntly, "I had a brain biopsy? Wasn't that dangerous?"

Well, yeah, it was dangerous, but I explained to him that I only consented after much consultation with doctors – there in Boston, in Connecticut and even family members who are well skilled in the medical profession.

Recently, Joe shared with me that he does remember waking up in the ICU after "something" and counted to ten to make sure he was ok. He also knew it was my birthday and, indeed, he was crying when I saw him because he was not able to celebrate the day with me.

June 14, 2016, 6:54PM

Hi dear friends and family,

We are in to Boston for Joe to consult with Dr. Jacobsen about the CLL.

We arrived last night and stayed at a local hotel to make the early morning doctor appointment more convenient for us. However, Joe woke up this morning slightly disoriented and his speech is worse. He is also having trouble with word retrieval (expressive aphasia).

This morning we got ourselves to Dana Farber to meet the oncologist – Dr. Eric Jacobsen – who turned out to be wonderful - well-informed and kind. We shared with him, of course, the changes in Joe since last night, including his speech difficulties.

After his initial CLL assessment and information sharing, Dr. Jacobsen insisted Joe be seen by a doctor in the ER at Brigham and Women's hospital. And, so we went, by ambulance, all the way across the street from the Dana Farber building to the hospital. Our first (and hopefully last) ambulance ride and it was about 100 feet).

He was admitted this evening.

Within all this anxiety there are, from rare time to time, humorous asides - such as when every time a doctor comes into the room he or she gives Joe the same "test"; having him hold his hands out, touching his nose, telling us what day/time/season it is and where he is. Sometimes he gets it right. Most of the time not.

I definitely knew we were dealing with something major when one of the doctors held his outstretched hand up in front of Joe to see. Wiggling his fingers slightly, he asked Joe what that was.

Without hesitation Joe said, "a fish." It was disturbing to hear, but so very hilarious.

Uh Oh, expressive aphasia (having trouble finding the right words) coming on strong!

I will keep you informed as we get information.

I am staying in his room tonight (I was able to wrangle a single room and a recliner chair for me), as there is not a hotel room available in town due to a convention.

Love yas,
Caryn

****

June 20, 2016, 8:50 PM

Dear friends and family,

Another fabulous doctor has come into our lives and that is Dr. Lakshmi Nayak, a neuro-oncologist who is instrumental in figuring out what the heck happened to poor Joe. She is kind, supportive and knowledgeable. With her input, we agreed to have Joe undergo a brain biopsy, which might give us some answers. At this point it is about the only option left.

So, today, on my birthday, the surgery took place. This was definitely not the birthday I had planned for myself, but my gift was that Joe made it through the brain biopsy.

We were both so very frightened – as were the kids, of course.

He's resting in ICU and I can't see him until the morning.

This is so surreal.

In the meantime, the kids took me to dinner for my birthday and even had a piece of lemon meringue pie with a candle in it for me - what a birthday this was. They even allowed me one espresso martini. One. They held their ground in not allowing me two. I sure could have used that second drink and a chance to have my head go somewhere else – anywhere but the reality of the moment.

Pls forgive me for emailing and not calling.
I am rather overwhelmed

Hugs, Caryn

June 23–27, 2015

On June 23, 2015, we left Canada and drove back to our vacation home in Vermont where, on the 27ᵗʰ, Joe participated in the Long Trail Century bike ride to raise money for Vermont Adaptive Ski and Sports in Killington, Vermont. I volunteered to help man a rest station for the riders while he cycled the 60-mile loop. He is a strong rider, but not fast, so he decided to do that shorter loop rather than the 100 miles that would have taken too long and he'd have missed the afternoon party. Good decision as the music and beer flowed freely along with the bar-b-que and conversations with the other participants.

We had bid on a brand new, high tech, exercise rowing machine in the silent auction. For some reason, we were the only ones to have placed a bid on it and, so, were able to stuff it into our car and bring it back home. I knew it was a great addition to our exercise equipment. I just didn't realize then how important it would be the following year as Joe would begin to regain his strength after his lengthy hospitalizations.

June 23, 2016, 8:42AM

Here's an update for you that might break the tension a bit. So, last night I stayed in Joe's room (again) and about 1:00 in the morning he got up from bed (by himself – which they said he could do) and went to the bathroom.

I watched from my perch on the reclining chair as he opened the bathroom door, stood there for a few seconds, closed the door and went back to bed.

I had to investigate.

Yup, as I had suspected, Joe in his medically-induced, hazy half-sleep, had used the bathroom to urinate. He just didn't think it necessary to make it all the way to the toilet.

Yes, I told the nurse who called housekeeping who sent a woman to come and clean up the mess.

Now I was wide-awake – which is a good thing cause as soon as the bathroom had been cleaned, Joe got up and did it again.

I can't wait till he's better and can see the humor in this.
Right now I am sleepy and fatigued and really, really annoyed!

Hugs,
Caryn

****

June 27, 2016, 6:46PM

Hi gang,

The word is good and hopeful. Joe was transferred to Spaulding Rehabilitation Hospital here in Boston today. Of course, I was given about 15 minutes notice to gather his things for the ambulance ride across town, and, so, true to form, I ended up leaving his reading glasses behind.

Oopsie.

Spaulding looks amazing – it is a top rehab hospital and, along with the care Joe got at Brigham and Women's, Dana Farber and now here, we feel fortunate that this whole chapter of our lives happened in Boston.

That's all for now,
Caryn

Chapter Six:
My Education in "Hospital"

"It's not the load that breaks you down. It's the way you carry it."
~Lena Horne

A good education is important – we all know that. From elementary school through college, we would bemoan having to get up early in the morning to attend class. As we moved through the grades, however, we began to discern the significance of that education and see how it would greatly enhance our future lives.

Once finished with our formal schooling, our learning never ends as we continue to absorb the knowledge that helps us thrive at our prospective careers and make the choices that will benefit us and those with whom we live and work.

I had thought about going back to school last year to finish the long overdue Master's Degree that I'd abandoned long ago.

Instead, I ended up getting an honorary (albeit unofficial) degree in "hospital."

I used the time in the hospital to begin my education – let's call it "Hospital 101" and those lessons I have learned helped me to cope – both physically and psychologically.

Watching the medical staff and being open to sharing my emotional life with my close friends and kids, taught me lessons that enabled me to help Joe through this difficult time. And, future struggles that I could not have known were ahead of us.

While Joe was being cared for by his doctors and nurses, I was busy soaking up any information I could get; from the reasons for and uses of each of his medications, learning to care for his catheter and feeding tube, making sure his head was not lower than a particular angle in bed, how to transfer him from that bed to a wheelchair, what foods were allowed on whichever dietary restrictions he had to follow at a particular time in his care.

It was fortunate that most of the staff welcomed my questions and were patient teachers. One kind doctor even referred to me as an important member of the team. Now, that was a very fine feeling.

The physical therapist, occupational therapist and speech therapist allowed me to shadow them, so I might know how to best help Joe when he came home.

There was much to learn. And, I soaked it up. I wish I had been such an avid student when I was younger – I might have my PhD by now.

But without garnering that knowledge everything "hospital" would have been a confusing blur and I am certain I'd not have been much of a help to Joe.

Late one morning, as I was making my way to the cafe, I happened upon a woman – about my age – wandering through the maze of corridors. Of course, I stopped and asked how I might help and she said she was looking for the cafe. I took her by the arm and together we walked to get our snacks.

Along the way, she told me how confusing it all was, how frustrated she became in trying to help her ailing husband. She did not understand what the staff was doing for him and, therefore, how she could be of help. This created a great deal of angst for her.

My reply, I think, unfortunately, came in the form of minor disbelief. "Don't you watch what's going on? Haven't you learned to work the system?"

Her blank stare in response told me that, no; she had not a clue about how anything worked. I also felt that she was slightly more "old school" in thinking she dare not meddle into the business of the medical staff.

I was not advising her to meddle into areas where she did not belong. Hopefully I, myself, have never done that and, had that happened, I felt the staff and I were open enough to have discussed that I overstep my boundaries. I believed I was not overstepping boundaries as I explained to this woman the importance of watching and studying the doctors and nurses to understand what procedures they are performing – and why it is medically advisable to do so. She also needed to learn the politics of the hospital; who tends to be in charge of her husband's case, to whom the others defer and to make sure that person includes her in the informational loop. When something is confusing, I suggested she shouldn't be shy in asking relevant questions. If one staff member is not open to her then she should find someone else to be her advocate. Patient advocates abound. So, too, are caregiver advocates – it is a matter of finding them.

The Resource section at the end of this book will help in your search.

What I did learn – and am still learning - about the medical system will stay with me for a long time so I can continue to help Joe as he continues to heal.

In a perfect hospital world, being part of "the team" as that particularly kind doctor proclaimed, would be the norm. But, this is not a perfect world and, therefore, from time to time, I had run into staff members who – to be blunt – rubbed me the wrong way.

There was the neurological resident who, standing at Joe's bedside and looking at a slight drooping of the mouth, proclaimed, "Oh, he is having a stroke!" That might have been so, but that surely wasn't something Joe needed to hear at that moment. I ushered him out of the room and let him know, in no uncertain terms, that I totally disagreed with his bedside manner.

But, also understanding that this is a man who is learning, and is also a man who is very kind and caring, I made sure the next day to address our misunderstanding and let him know I was commenting on his technique – not his character. After a warm handshake, we were on the same page again.

Several weeks later, after he was moved to another rotation in the hospital, I came upon him in the cafeteria, sitting alone, munching on a piece of pizza. I went over to him to say hello and asked how he was doing. He pointed to the seat across from him and invited me to join him and then said, very sincerely, "I have a lot to learn."

We both did.

There was the doctor who didn't think Joe was a good candidate for the hospital's rehab section and he made me more than angry – I was furious at his behavior and attitude. But, once again, I had to remember that his decision was not based on a personal vendetta against Joe; he just did not know Joe's strength of character and tenacity. Once apprised of these virtues, he relented and allowed Joe to enter the program.

We stayed cordial knowing we both wanted the best for our patient.

Do I always like the manner and/or decisions made by those who are caring for my husband? No. Absolutely not. These are folks who are in positions of power having greater medical knowledge than I possess, however, they are certainly not gods. They can make mistakes, just like any of us. Their approach to particular problems might not make sense to me, but they deserve my indulgence as I examine their actions against my reactions.

And, if we still disagree, duking it out with them does me – and, therefore, Joe – no good. Engaging in an acrimonious relationship with the people who are there to help Joe get better will only make the process more difficult for all involved.

There was only one time I requested Joe not have a particular nurse. Joe's medications, at times, made him anxious and - sorry Joe - ornery. Their personalities clashed so greatly that I was concerned it would become contentious. We most certainly didn't need that to happen.

Was I close to exploding from time to time? I sure was. But somehow the saner part of me found a way to escape an all-out, duke-it-out, conflict.

When that seemed to be looming, I would walk out of the room, and into the café for a bag of maple bacon potato chips (By the way, you haven't lived, if you've never had a bag of these amazing chips – I have now become addicted). Or, I'd go into the family room and sit quietly doing yoga breathing. Or, call a friend or my kids and rant about the staff member to them.

Or, as I am doing right now, writing about being chill when what I'd rather do is rant.

I have been in the hospital when other caregivers were screaming at a staff member and wonder just how effective that outburst is. I'd say it isn't going to bring about an understanding and, therefore, a united front in caring for the patient.

We each have our part to play and, when we disagree, as difficult as it is at times, we need to hide our egos, listen to each other, learn from each other, and remember the ultimate goal is to bring the patient back to good health.

My "honorary" degree in "hospital" has held me in good stead. I just hope I never have to use it again.

Chapter Seven:
The Healing Had Just Begun

~July~

July 1-12, 2015

It was on July 10, 2015, that Joe and I set off to visit Niagara Falls. With all his world travels, that was one place he'd never seen and, as we were on our way upstate for a bike ride around the Erie Canal, it seemed sensible to fill in this blank in his travel diary. With the two friends who were going to join us on the bike ride, we spent an evening "oohing" and "aahing" over the spectacular views, even as we found our way around the multitude of other tourists who joined us in our appreciation of the wondrous piece of natural beauty. The falls, that is. Not the surrounding tourist traps and tacky stores that tried to vie, unsuccessfully, for our attention.

Sunday the 12th, Joe and his friend met up with the fifty other cyclists who were about to ride the trails around the Erie Canal. Our friend's wife and I also saw the sights on wheels – however, ours were attached to the car, as neither she nor I are comfortable on a bike. At the end of each day, we all met back at whatever campsite was next on the trail, set up our tents, cleaned up in the shower truck and bedded down to rest for whatever adventures awaited us the next day. On the 19th, the trip was completed, and I was ready for the drive back home and a real shower.

On July 19th of the next year we had also just come back home - but not from a bike ride.

July 1, 2016, 9:45AM

Dear friends and family,

We just got the word that the brain biopsy showed CLL cells had created the strokes. They are not sure how/why. It is a great mystery and extremely rare.

Leave it to Joe to do something extremely rare!

In the meantime, he has rebounded amazingly well and quickly. Every day there is a great new improvement in his ability to communicate and walk.

It is a great relief to see him progress to this point.

Spaulding Rehab is very special, helping folks with so many major physical challenges. Yet, when the patients are in the gym they are all smiling and cheering themselves and each other when progress – however minute – is attained.

Love you all
Caryn

****

July 4, 2016, 2:20PM

Happy 4th of July everyone! It is especially joyful here as the lunch for today was a hot dog and apple pie. You should have seen Joe smile as he downed some of his favorite treats. We have a photo of him with that hotdog half-in and half-out of his mouth. Looks pretty much like a cigar and is a very funny pic.

Thankfully, we have gotten to the point where we can laugh and start to relax.

The stuff that is holding Joe back, however, are those things he loves to do most, work on his computer and read a good book. He doesn't have the attention span to read.

And, using his electronic devices is a quandary for him. The occupational therapist has shown me an app that we can use here, and when Joe gets home, that might help him. But, wow, to see him so confused is upsetting.

Hugs
Caryn

July 6,2016, 8:34AM

OMG! I walked into Joe's room today to find him using his iPad! Yow!

Ain't the brain an amazing thing!!!!

That's all for now – I'm going to go get a cup of coffee and some oatmeal from the cafeteria downstairs and celebrate. Maybe even one of their yummy, greasy donuts.

Love
Caryn

****

July 10, 2016, 4:54PM

We went for a bike ride!!!!!!!!!

They have recumbent, three-wheel bikes and Joe was asked if he wanted to take a ride on one around the hospital property. Of course, he did!!!!!!

I was invited to join the expedition, as well.

What a blast we had, and how marvelous it was to see Joe on a bike again. He was beaming, as was I, as was the staff members who went with us.

Yahoooooooo,
Love you all
Caryn

****

July 12, 2016, 9:08PM

Dear caring family and friends,

Well, we are on the home stretch - literally.

Today Joe had his community outing to the zoo-the first time in a month that he has been outside for an extended period of time.

He did well, walking around and enjoying the company of the two other patients who were on the adventure with him.

I did not go with him: he does not need me shadowing him everywhere. But I hear he had ice cream (a treat denied to him before this as it was difficult for him to swallow) and I wish I was there just to see the grin on his face as he scarfed down this special treat).

That's all for now,
Caryn

July 18- 25, 2015

On July 22, 2015, we were back home after the cycling trip around the Erie Canal with stories to share with family and friends about our adventures.

However, fast-forwarding to 2016 discloses that we had been home from Boston just a week and were settling in nicely with Joe continuing his speech, occupational and physical therapy at Danbury Hospital's outpatient rehabilitation facility. There were various doctor appointments on our schedule and, as Joe wasn't driving yet, it was on me to take him to these sessions several times a week.

But we were fine, happy to be back in our own house and it was easy to care for Joe, for his special needs were few.

We were busy planning our annual Golden Family Reunion that was to be held (again) at our house on the 30th of the month. But, things don't always pan out as you have planned, as we discovered within a week of our homecoming.

First, however, Joe needed his next round of chemo and we decided to go back up to Boston to have the infusion.

Jul 18, 2016, 3:42AM,

Hi all,

We are settling in back home nicely and really don't need any help. The things that Joe needs help with are getting to relearn the computer and other cognitive tasks.

He's not driving yet and so I'm taking him to various places -but these are only the first few days home and so, we will figure out a schedule.

His therapies take place at Danbury Hospital outpatient therapy and we're going to the first few sessions this morning and then tomorrow.

On Wednesday, I really need to get my haircut as it is now far too long and so one of Joe's friends will come take him out to lunch so I can get to the hairstylist.

And now we are off early this morning for the first of the therapy sessions.

Love you much,
Caryn

****

July 22, 2016, 12:47PM

Dear friends and family,

Joe and I came back up to Boston yesterday for the first of two of this round of chemo infusions and is now at Brigham and Women's emergency dept. and will be admitted to a regular room.

This morning he was terribly weak and disoriented. We were on our way to the hospital for the second infusion and barely made it over here. His blood pressure is extremely low and his fever very high. The doctor's say it might be chemo related but probably not and they feel he might have sepsis.

Joe is extremely upset, agitated and only wants to bust out of here. This is making is so very difficult on me as I agree with the doctors that we have to play it safe and keep him here a few days.

Love
Caryn

****

July 25, 2016, 6:52PM,

Hi, it's me again,

We are home. After a weekend of being given high doses of IV antibiotics, Joe's fever abated, and his blood pressure is okay.

It was not sepsis after all and most likely a reaction to the chemo.

Dang!

But at least that is now behind us and we can get back to our lives, which include the annual Golden family party on Sunday.

We will not cancel. It will be a long day for Joe, but we both recognize that we need something celebratory in our lives right now.

Love you
Caryn

Chapter Eight:
Caregiver, Soothe Thyself

"Nurturing yourself is not selfish – it is essential to our survival and your well-being."
~Renee Peterson Trudeau

While in Boston, I felt it my duty to be at Joe's bedside 12 hours a day, every day. There were even nights when I curled up in the lounge chair next to his bed and tried, in vain, to sleep through the beeping of Joe's infusion pumps, the nurses' interruptions to take his vital signs and my own worry about his well-being. In the few hours I allowed myself to be away at my hotel room, I would accomplish one task a day. Perhaps, I did my laundry, or sorted through the mail our kids had brought with them when they visited so I could sit in Joe's room the next day and pay the bills.

I felt I needed to be with him to make sure that the medical staff was on top of things, that the nurses and aides gave him the right medication at the proper times and that the head of his bed was raised sufficiently when he was receiving nutrition through the feeding tube.

In other words, I was the caregivers' caregiver. It was all on my shoulders.

And, my shoulders were just barely strong enough for the weight they were carrying.

All my caring friends and family members were concerned about me and kept insisting that I take care of myself.

"Get help," they all told me. "You need professional guidance," my family and friends chanted as I navigated this unfamiliar chapter in our lives.

"Not necessary," I responded vehemently. Give guidance, that's what I do for a living. I work with women and girls on dealing with life's challenges. I know what to do; I'll simply employ the principals of the Tao, breathe deeply, and meditate—and I'll be just fine. Well, and maybe I'll swallow a few Ativan from time to time.

"Please," they continued, "even if you think you know it all, there might be someone out there with a new point of view for you."

"Go speak to someone even to prove us all wrong," they continued.

Aha! That was the challenge I could not refuse.

So, during one of Joe's long hospitalizations, I met with the social worker in the facility's caregiver center. She was lovely, kind, caring, smart, and offered many helpful suggestions — but none that I had not already come up with myself.

Well, maybe a few tidbits of information and, I had to admit, hearing her words validated and enhanced what I was already doing. She, and her point of view, gave me some measure of comfort.

I thanked everyone for pushing me; told them I was doing fine and now, "Please get off my back."

They were right, but even with all their fine suggestions there was no way I could focus on my own well-being. I just didn't know how.

I had remained by his side all day, every day for, to not be there, meant, to me, that I was deserting him. In the words of a very wise friend, deserting Joe would have meant flying off to Lake Como with George Clooney, not going around the block for a walk or getting my hair cut. Okay, so I was most certainly not deserting Joe, but I was absolutely neglecting my own needs.

It took a volcanic meltdown for me to grasp that I was not omnipotent and needed to take time and space to replenish my depleted body and soul.

I am not talking about the "need" to get my hair and nails done. I am referring to taking the time to be with friends who offered to come to Boston and take me to lunch. I am referring to taking a walk around the block and exercising my weary body. And, I am referring to leaving the hospital room in the evening, going to a hotel and getting a decent night's sleep to wake refreshed and ready to take on a new day of challenges.

Rather, I remained resolutely calm, controlled and clinical. I knew I could not — should not — cry, be upset or throw a tantrum in front of Joe. What he most needed was my strength and love. And, that was true.

But in reality, what I most needed was to cry, be angry, frightened and frustrated when I was away from him. I clung instead to being strong and not letting those feelings surface — ever — not with friends, not with our kids, not even with myself.

Then one evening, I erupted like Vesuvius.

I phoned one of my closest friends and sobbed uncontrollably as I walked from the hospital to my hotel. While still on the phone, I stopped in at a CVS to pick up some medications I expected would be waiting for me. When I discovered that the pharmacy was closed, I cursed like a crazy woman was inhabiting my body. My friend on the phone heard all of it. And, she must have been nodding and perhaps pleased that I had finally allowed my emotions to come out.

They should have been expressed sooner. I should have allowed myself the anger, frustration, concern and sadness, rather than assuming I was robotic and above those very human feelings.

It took an eruption of tears and rage (not to mention an apple martini and piece of chocolate cake) to teach me that I am mortal and vulnerable. And, that I, too, need to consciously release those feelings or they will burst out as they did in Vesuvian tears and distasteful behavior. It was not a pretty lesson, but I learned — or began learning — that it's okay — no, it's imperative! — to take care of myself physically, emotionally and mentally, while taking care of Joe.

Caregivers of the world, heed these words before you, too, are transformed into a volcano. Most certainly, it is not the best way to heal your fractured soul.

Chapter Nine:
The Situation Turns Dire

~August, September ~

August 2015

By August of 2015, Joe had been in the midst of his training for the upcoming Southern Tier bike ride to occur the following month. But, he took a short break when our hiking buddies came from hither and yon to join us in Vermont. It made for a great weekend – even when we did get lost on one of our convoluted hiking trails. So, of course, we made plans to all be together the following year.

However, in August of 2016, hiking with our friends was the furthest thought from our minds as Joe began to lose his ability to walk, to talk, to eat. We were losing him – or so we thought.

August 1, 2016, 4:47PM

Hi Hiking Buddies,

We are still hoping that Joe will be well enough for your visit to VT at the end of August. We did host the annual Golden Family party Saturday, but Joe had to take several naps throughout the day.

I will keep you updated – but at this point, know that we are still hoping for a fun few days with you all.

Sending you much love
Caryn

****

August 2, 2016, 1:32PM

Hi all,

We visited our local oncologist – Dr. Rella – this morning and he has been in touch with the oncologist – Dr. Jacobsen – in Boston.

They both feel confident that Joe can have his next chemo treatment in Danbury. It is scheduled for Wed and Thurs August 17 and 18th.

The medication that he has not yet had – the Rituxan, which helps the chemo's efficiency, will be administered the following week – Wed. August 24.

Love you all
Mom/Caryn

****

August 17, 2016, 5:54PM

Dear caring family and friends,

Joe did well today although the main problem was finding a vein that was not scarred over from all the other punctures he's had over the last several months. Therefore, it was decided that he should have a port inserted (just under the skin on his upper chest) – which will happen this coming Monday, the 22nd.

Next Wednesday will be Rituxan and, after that infusion, he'll be halfway done.

We continue to be impressed with the staff and facility at Danbury Hospital.

And now, we shall both relax as neither of us slept last night – he due to the steroids he received as one of the pre-medications, and me, well, 'cause he didn't.

Love you all,
Caryn

****

August 18, 2016, 7:53AM

This morning he is very weak, red all-over, maybe had fever through the night and had a headache - but he is telling everyone he didn't get sick and is fine – I guess compared to last time, he really is fine.

It would be unreasonable to assume he wouldn't get some reaction to the chemo.

Love you all
Caryn

****

August 19, 2016, 12:32PM

Not looking good – Joe had 102.1 fever last night, low blood pressure, chills.

This morning temp and BP ok but he was very unsteady on his feet, so we went to the emergency dept. at the hospital where a very good and kind doctor checked him out and sent us home – as long as I monitor his temp and blood pressure.

We shall have to come up with a way to deal with this chemo side effect should it happen again. I certainly can't not call the doctor, but we also can't have Joe spend his time in emergency rooms getting punctured for blood tests and IVs. We'll discuss it with Dr. Rella when we see him, I believe, on Wednesday before the Rituxan.

Love you all
Caryn

****

Aug 24, 2016, at 8:52 PM

Dear friends and family,

Things are not good here.
We got Joe to the emergency room at 3:30 this morning for major leg pain during the day yesterday that continued through last night.

One of the oncologists on call said we needed to come here. They put him on IV Dilaudid, gave him some oral meds and sent him home 9 hours later.

But, the pain came back with a vengeance and we are now back at the hospital where they will admit him, so they can control the pain.

Poor Joe, this is so yucky

Love to all
Caryn

****

August 26, 2016, 1:35:18PM

Dear friends and family,

Dr. Rella came, sat a long time and talked. Had already put in a call to Dana Farber. They want Joe to stay in hospital till they figure out what the heck is going on.

The Gabapentin has worked, and he has pain but now has to get Dilaudid out of his system for he is so weak from that, and extremely disoriented and, well, hallucinating.

Physical therapy has to assess him, as he is too weak to walk or stand. Neurologist came in but not oncology yet.

He just can't stand without his legs buckling under him even with people helping him and using a walker. Obviously, he can't come home.

Love to all
Caryn

****

August 27, 2016, 10:27AM

Dear all,

The update is not good. He is very confused and agitated. They just gave him Xanax and he is sleeping. Still can't walk. Kept trying to get out of bed all night. When I came he was in a chair seat-belted with a tray, so he couldn't get out. Also, disoriented which might still be the effects of the Dilaudid but to rule out (hopefully) another stroke they just did a CT scan (showed nothing) and will do an MRI tomorrow.

****

August 30, 2016, 7:17PM

Dear friends and family,

Joe was moved to the oncology floor and had the MRI of the spine and the spinal tap today. We should get those results tomorrow.

Very, very, very weak, can barely talk. Nothing new with the legs that don't move. He is less responsive.

Brain MRI showed cancer cells in the blood vessels creating the blockage that is damaging to his brain.

Eyes open from time to time, don't know what he knows. Is aware at some level. I walked into the room and put Purell on my hand and he reached out to me to put it on his hand. That is what we were doing in the past. It showed memory but more reflex.

They had to give him oxygen for labored breathing. Now, there is no leg movement at all and no speech at all.

Tomorrow, he will be given an infusion of a different chemo drug. We are hoping that this will end the progression of the nerve damage and, maybe even reverse it.

Doc said I should stay with Joe tonight, not that he expects the worst, but, if anything should happen, he knows I would want to be here. When I asked if Joe will be okay, the best the doc could say was, "I hope so."

Love to all, Caryn

September 2015

On September 10, of 2015, we were finally on our way to San Diego for the adventure that Joe had prepared for all year. He was to embark on the cycling trip with Adventure Cycling, (so aptly named) which would take him from there to St. Augustine, Florida. It seemed a daunting expedition but, as in the past, he would conquer these difficult miles and arrive at his destination with a flourish. We spent a glorious night at the Hotel Del Coronado, then several days with cousins, and finally, checked into the hostel where Joe met the cyclists with whom he was going to pedal his way across the country.

I was so very excited for Joe to embark on this next biking trip, even though it meant he would be on the road until the end of November. I loved that he had that in his life and pray that he will be able to experience a cycling adventure again one day.

September 2, 2016, 8:51PM

Hi all,

In trying to help Joe communicate I took a big sheet of paper and put each letter of the alphabet on it for him to point to the letters. No go. Didn't work. He had no idea what to do.

But hysterically, one of the staff members – trying to help - came into the room with the same idea and he held up his piece of paper with letters and he said, "suppose you want to say you are constipated, all you do is point to the C O. N. S, hmmmmm where is the S? Oh, there it is, T, I "

He had to use constipated??? He couldn't have used a three-letter word????

The guy is very caring but, yow, this was hysterical.

Love to all, Caryn

September 3, 2016, 5:44PM

Today Joe had a catheter inserted and began dialysis. His kidneys are not failing but are not working well enough to remove the chemo from his system.

He still can't swallow, so tonight he started getting nutrition through his catheter. We are hoping this is short term, so they won't have to insert a feeding tube.

Poor guy was put through the mill today and, so, when I left him tonight, he was extremely tired.

The good news is that he moved his left leg a bit. That was exciting to see. And his right arm and hand were able to move more easily and higher.

I arrive each morning assuming I will see some improvement and that has been the case each day. Tiny steps forward, but they are steps forward and that is good.

Love to all
Caryn

****

September 7, 2016, 9:31AM

Dear caring friends and family,

This morning Joe called me on my way to the hospital, one of the nurses dialed for him. I understood him say "hello" and "I love you".

I almost broke down and cried.

Love you all
Caryn

September 10, 2016, 6:21PM

Hi all,

Well, Google tells me that the wildest roller coaster ride in the country is in Jersey at Six Flags Amusement Park.

I disagree. The wildest roller coaster ride is at Danbury Hospital, room 18, on the 11th floor.

Yesterday Joe was running a fever of 103.6, which then dropped to 101.2. His blood pressure has been low, and he is sleeping and extremely weak again. They put him on a broad-spectrum antibiotic until blood cultures and tests come back with the reason for the fever.

****

I arrived this morning to find a very pale Joe lying on a cooling blanket in his bed. Without the ability to give him Tylenol, the cooling blanket was the only choice to bring the fever down.

At one point, there was a concern about a specific infection and he was put on isolation for several hours until that was, thankfully, ruled out.

His platelets were extremely low so they had to infuse platelets in the morning and will do so again this evening. He had had a transfusion last night and then again during dialysis his afternoon. Things were looking pretty bleak.

But, about an hour ago he came back from dialysis awake, alert and talking clearly enough for me to understand most of what he was saying.

Wow. Is this man driving me nuts!

Love to all
Caryn

****

September 11, 2016, 5:56PM

After yesterday's difficult day, I did not know what to expect when I arrived in Joe's room this morning so got there earlier than usual expecting, anything.

The man I saw lying in Joe's bed sure wasn't the lethargic Joe from yesterday. Today, he was replaced by an agitated man who was raring to go home and didn't understand why he can't yet.

Joe has been chomping at the bit to get out of bed – understandable – but not something he can do yet. Therefore, hopefully, to get him to understand why we won't let him get up I asked a gal from PT to and help Joe sit up for a few minutes. Then she let him try to get out of bed and he, of course, could not do that.

I figured he now understood – but, nope, as soon as she left Joe was rolling over and trying to get out of bed! When I stopped him (yet again) and explained that he can't do that yet, he looked at me and in a voice that should be reserved for someone running from a bear, yelled, "Bitch!"

I'm sure one day I'll find that funny but right now it stings.

Love to all, Caryn

****

September 13, 2016, 4:09PM

A quick update before I fall asleep in this chair in Joe's room:

Joe slept much of today and yesterday. Today partly due to the pain meds he is on as his mouth sores are extremely painful. That is one of the awful side effects of the chemo he was given a few weeks ago.

Joe will need another transfusion of platelets as his number has dipped down again. The cancer cells invade the bone marrow and mess with blood production.

As I am reading this back, I see it is as a good news/bad news sort of report, so let's end with good stuff. Joe's kidneys are working well once again and he will not need any more dialysis. Hooray for these positive steps forward!

Hugs to all, Caryn

September 16, 2016, 6:14PM

My dear friends and family,

The nurses got him sitting in a chair for a short time today - as Joe really has no strength to get himself up, they used something called a Hoya Lift. It's an interesting contraption that puts a sling under Joe and supports him much like being in a swing seat.

His red blood cells are low - making him anemic, therefore he will get a transfusion this evening.

He still isn't really eating other than the few spoonsful of thickened water, pudding or pureed fruit I can get him to swallow.

And, that's the scoop from room 18 tonight.

Thank you for you continued outpouring of caring, love and support.
Caryn

****

September 20, 2016, 10:23AM

Good morning all,

Sitting at Joe's bedside as he slumbers comfortably. He was given morphine to help ease the pain of those sores on his back as they continue to heal with the help of the wound-care specialist here.

I met the nutritionist today and we are going to monitor his food intake, which, at this point, is very little. But, she will try to introduce some Ensure to help get his calories up. The hope, of course, is to get Joe off the IV nutrition.

He was very bright and alert this morning when I arrived and looked pretty good.

The oncologist will start Joe on another chemo drug. This one is taken orally, three a day, every day, for the rest of Joe's life. This means that he will have that constant dose to keep the CLL at bay. He'll start that by the end of this week or early next week. And, he will start on a lower dose to insure that there aren't too many side effects. I like that Joe will still be in the hospital when he begins the chemo, so he can be monitored.

That is all I can think of at this point.

I have loved all your caring emails and thank you so very much.

Hugs to all, Caryn

****

September 23, 2016, 3:48PM

The saga of Joe and his unlikely and unwanted and uninvited CLL continues and things continue to look up.

Joe's liver and kidney functions continue to improve, his body is infection-free, and the antibiotic's will soon be removed, and the strength and mobility in his hand and legs are coming along nicely - although his right leg and foot still refuse to make any great progress.

This morning began with a ride to the local FedEx to pick up Joe's new chemo, which is in pill form and will be taken three at a time, once a day, every day, for life. It is actually not a chemo drug, but is one of the newer forms of drugs called targeted therapy. According to my research on "Dr. Google", targeted cancer therapies are drugs or other substances that block the growth and spread of cancer by interfering with specific molecules ("molecular targets") that are involved in the growth, progression, and spread of cancer.

According to the fact sheet that came with the drug, there can be numerous side effects. According to Joe's oncologist, they are all very rare.

He was assessed by one of the doctors from the rehab team here and deemed not strong enough to be moved to the rehab floor, which is 7 South here at the hospital.

Another assessment will be made next week. It is our hope that soon Joe will be strong enough to undergo the rigorous rehab schedule they have here, for this is the only place we would want him to be once he leaves the hospital setting.

And, that is the news for today. I shall update you when we know how well Joe tolerates the new drug.

Hugs to all, Caryn

September 27, 2016, 3:00PM

Hi dear family and friends,

Yesterday afternoon, the team recognized it was time to give Joe a feeding tube to supplement the small amount of nutrition he is getting with his poor eating.

When I first saw it, my mind went immediately to something out of the movie "Alien." I was afraid Joe would be upset when he first saw it, so I stayed with him in the hospital overnight last night.

However, on the eating end of things, this morning Joe told me that he wanted a donut. And so, when the speech and swallow specialist appeared on the floor about half an hour ago, I told him and, while it certainly was not part of the puréed diet that Joe has been forced to eat - or rather not eat - for the last five weeks, the therapist ran down to the café and appeared with a chocolate and sprinkle covered donut that Joe promptly devoured.

It is possible that Joe will be discharged from the hospital by the end of this week, so thought is going into where he will go next. He and I would like him to be here in the hospital on their rehab floor, but in order to go there, and to be admitted, he has to show that he can do the three hours of intensive therapy a day.

And so, I called in all my contacts and had Paul Badger, head of inpatient PT and Jeff McKay – who had been my therapist when I had been here - come assess Joe and work with him. The rehab area is 7 South and that's where I did my rehab two years ago, so I know quite a few people there. And, I guess I behaved well back then because Paul came right up to work with Joe when I asked. Together they will advocate for Joe remaining in this facility for his therapy.

It's our hope that if he works with Joe for the next four or five days Joe will show that he has the strength, stamina and the will to work hard and they will admit him to 7 South.

Love and hugs to you all,
Caryn

September 30, 2016, 9:19AM

Good morning all,

Joe tried to eat his breakfast but said, loud and clear, "It tastes like shit."

I will be bringing him his meals from the cafe from now on.

Hugs
Caryn

Chapter Ten:
Those Hidden Cracks

They are often there, those hidden cracks in the foundation. We don't see them; we assume we are standing on strong and steady ground until the day there is an upheaval. And, the infrastructure collapses.

Much like the bonds with family and friends.

And, I've recently discovered many of those bonds to be far weaker than I formerly believed.

When Joe had suffered two strokes within a few weeks, there was an outpouring of love, and support from the folks in our lives who truly care. Their calls, texts, cards, letters, gifts of flowers and balloons, and food when we came home (we shall be eating lasagna and pot pies for a very long time), became the bedrock upon which we were able to continue on through the batteries of tests that Joe had to endure while in the hospital.

Those caring family members and friends were also ready to bolster me through the caregiving process. They allowed me to call them as I cried, ranted or merely conversed and held tight to their companionship.

But, unfortunately, some cracks began to appear in the foundation — a foundation that I had always believed to be unfaltering.

Friends who I had assumed would be there for us simply disappeared. There was little or no contact from them. It was strange and disconcerting. Where were these people who had always been in our lives? Is this what is meant by "fair weather friends"? People who remain by your side only when life is good and happy and not complicated? Yes, that appears to be the case.

And, there are those who truly want to be in touch, yet simply don't know how to reach out – as happened one day on my way to the hospital. I had stopped at the mailbox in front of the local deli and encountered a friend who was on his way into the store.

We stopped. He stopped. We exchanged hellos and then, positioning his facial features like the ultimate emoji for "contrite," our friend mumbled a litany of excuses for not having been in touch through the last few months of Joe's illness.

He was out of town. He was busy with the grandkids. He didn't want to intrude into our lives at this challenging time. But, he most certainly did care and hoped all was well.

The thing is, I didn't need to hear his rationalizations for not contacting us. Quite honestly, at that moment of our chance meeting, I was quite amused by his fumbling excuses. This is a kind man and for whatever reasons he couldn't be in touch with us — I really didn't care.

What I cared about was knowing that he had followed Joe's progress through our mutual friends and that he looked truly relieved to see Joe looking so fine when we bumped into him at the deli.

He was looking for vindication for the indiscretion of not calling yet, there was nothing to forgive. Nor was there forgiveness to be doled out when another friend called recently and began her conversation with, "I know I haven't called sooner, but I have been in touch with our friends, and I realized it was about time I called you because I want you to know that I care."

Wow, that was quite a mouthful. And, again, so unnecessary. There she was, on the phone, talking to me and inquiring about both Joe and me and our progress. And, it was apparent that she had been kept in the loop. Of course, she cared. And, she dialed the phone to connect with Joe and me. That meaningful act meant the world to us.

Most of these folks all mean well and we, who are privy to the backpedaling, can chose to get ourselves into a tizzy about their seemingly lack of caring, or take them at their word — circumstances created the void in contact.

Being the idealist who always sees the best in folks, I have chosen to remember that we all have burdens. It is quite impossible to put aside our own circumstances to fully concentrate on others. And, that does not mean we don't care about those others. It means we are human and can juggle just so many priorities at a time.

Yet, I forgive them their inattention. I understand it is difficult for many to deal with adversity, and often people are so entwined in their own affairs they have no energy for others.

And, that is all right, for I have always believed that we have friends on several levels; those who are there for the party side of life — the ones with whom we can share a meal and enjoy a laugh of two — and those who are there for the long haul, as together we bolster each other up through life's complexities.

But as the foundation of Joe's and my lives had started to unravel, the truly deep fissures were beginning to appear.

And, the greatest cracks in the foundation came from the most unexpected place - family members.

Two weeks after having arrived home from the hospital, Joe and I hosted our annual family party. This is a tradition we were determined to not abandon. Yes, Joe was exhausted and had to retire to a bedroom for a nap from time to time during the afternoon, but seeing our cousins, children and grandchildren was the most uplifting tonic he could have taken. And, allowing these loving people to spend time with Joe brought them much joy.

It was a beautiful afternoon, one that would have been perfect if not for those dang awful cracks in the foundation; the people who were not with us, had not responded to the invitation, and had never been in contact with us through Joe's ordeal.

While talking to one of our cousins, I began to criticize those who abandoned Joe when he most needed their support. It was unconscionable that they disappeared and did not contact us in any manner to reach out with caring and love. My cousin told me about the bridge that appears just fine - until there is a stressor that allows the hidden cracks to show.

There were, indeed, hidden cracks in the infrastructure of our family.

As there might very well be in your family, when the foundation of your life is shaken.

My suggestion is to accept that these folks can only do so much; can only behave in the manner that works for them; can only love and support others to extent of their capability. We cannot ask any more than that of them. And, we either forgive or harbor a resentment that harms our own souls. Forgiving heals the cracks far more successfully than resentment.

I chose to forgive. And, am grateful for the bedrock of our family and friends — those who were, and always will be, there for us. As Joe and I will be for them.

Chapter Eleven:
Out of the Hospital

~October~

October 2015

I flew into Austin the morning of October 18, 2015 and watched Joe and the group ride into the city for a rest day. I went to the hostel where they are all staying for two nights to watch the grand entrance of the bikes. Joe and I, however, are staying at a hotel near here – I want a bit more splendor for my biker dude and me once we are together for two nights after five weeks apart.

He was having the most fabulous time – I can't imagine peddling over the mountains, setting up a tent (or in Joe's case – when they are in a park he just puts his sleeping bag on a picnic table). It had been a tough ride, but he was persevering and strong and tenacious.

Those three traits held Joe in good stead and helped him overcome the ravages of the CLL and his strokes.

October 1, 2016, 11:51AM

Hi everyone,

Well it was just yesterday morning that I was stressing over a placement for Joe when he was discharged from the hospital. And it was yesterday afternoon that we were told he would be moved to 7 South, the outstanding rehab right here in the hospital. And shortly after that he was, indeed, brought to his new "home" in the hospital in the rehab facility.

This morning showed us that without a doubt this is where Joe needs to be and why our friends in PT were fighting so hard to keep him here.

Jeff McKay started out by getting Joe into a wheelchair, bringing him to the gym and having him stand at the parallel bars. Jeff probably did 90% of work, but the 10% that Joe's leg strength aided in having him stand was a huge accomplishment.

And as Joe was standing there, Jeff looked him in the eyes and said Joe was the strongest and most determined man he knows and that is why he fought so hard to get him to 7 South. Jeff, Joe and I know that if there is any chance of Joe working his way back from this devastating situation, it will happen here.

And today I saw that Joe will make great strides and I am no longer frightened.

I have learned – as of yesterday – that I do need to take care of myself more than I had been doing. And it is all right, for Joe is now in a place where he doesn't need me every minute to direct his care. I probably didn't need to direct his care before, either, but I had to do it for that was all I could do to help him. Wow – I think that is a topic for another blog. :-)

Love to you all, Caryn

****

October 10, 2016, 8:35AM

Hello all,

I am now planning for Joe's homecoming, which they state might be as soon as Oct 21. But both Jeff and I understand that Joe might not be ready, and I am all geared up to fight to keep Joe longer. At least until he can transfer from bed to chair himself - with the help of someone. I will not let him need a Hoyer lift to get from bed to chair.

He needs to be able to transfer from bed to chair, to be off the Foley catheter and feeding tube - if possible.

I have insisted that I be allowed to attend one of the team meetings for Joe - I am, after all, an integral part of the team. That will take place on Thursday.

Love to all, Caryn

October 13, 2016, 8:59PM

My dear caring friends and family,

I had the family meeting today and I was extremely disappointed – the team and I could not get a word in edgewise to suggest that we petition Medicare to keep Joe an extra week for medical reasons.

No go. Joe will leave 7 South on Friday, October 21.

When he is discharged the feeding tube, the catheter, the horrific bedsore wound will all still be there.

And he won't be any easier to transfer so Jeff is helping me find alternative transfer equipment rather than the Hoyer lift.

There is so much to plan and do before we bring him home in just eleven days.

I came home right after the meeting and met with the guy who is going to install the ramps to get Joe from the garage to the house and from the kitchen level to the bedroom/family room level.

I have spoken to the nursing agency and she has an aide ready to live here with us – a gal who is highly regarded and trusted. She is also willing to learn to help with the catheter and feeding tube – this is a huge help.

Tomorrow morning, I will touch base with a trusted home health agency to set a schedule for OT, PT, speech, and visiting nurses. I'm also working on getting the hospital bed in the house. My friend is loaning us a wheelchair and a transport wheelchair, and I will get it from her next week or maybe over the weekend.

I have not waited for the case manager on the floor to arrange for an ambulette to bring him home as I was given the name of a private person who will be a great help to us not only in getting him home, but getting him into the house once we are there.

Have I missed anything? I don't think so, but if you see any piece missing from this puzzle please let me know.

Love you all, Caryn

****

October 15, 2016, 3:44PM

Happy Saturday (and it is, indeed, happy)

Joe has recently been given permission to intake thin liquids, which also includes frozen foods that melt into thin liquids - like ice cream, like his very favorite flavor from our local creamery, Bada Bing! And, so, we had an ice cream party today in the patient lounge as we enjoyed the Bada Bing (chocolate cream with chunks of dark chocolate and bing cherries) we brought in from the local creamery.

So much fun!

As Joe's medical problems begin to settle down and as his physical disabilities slowly improve, it is exciting to plan for his homecoming.

Joe had spent much of the past 7 1/2 weeks in a fog but this week he has come back to us, is speaking again, is cognitively aware and continues to work hard at his therapies.

Biker Joe is back, and I am beyond thrilled.

I thank you all for caring so much-your outpouring of love has helped tremendously in getting us both to this point.

Sending love and hugs
Caryn

****

October 18, 2016, 9:2PM

As of last week, Joe started coming back to us: his speech was clearer, glimmers of his upbeat and fun personality began to appear. And by this week the Joe we all know and love - with his sharp mind and sweet sense of humor - is back in full force.

This has been a long and arduous haul but today, when he walked the length of the parallel bars in the therapy gym (his physical therapist holding him up and sharing words of encouragement), Joe was able to move his legs forward by himself. What a thrill for everyone on the rehab floor to see. Especially Joe, who, rather than bemoaning the fact that he had to work so hard to walk, was overwhelmed at the fact that he could achieve this amazing feat.

And, now we look forward to his continued healing at home. As Joe said, it will be lots of work, but we are both ready for this next stage of our new normal and it will be so wonderful to be back in the house together again!

I suspect the next update from me will be with Joe sitting next to me in the house. Maybe not as soon as we get home, but once again, if you don't hear from me for a little while, please know all is good. I am just rather busy.

Love and hugs to you all,
Caryn

****

October 22, 2016, 1:32PM

Dear all,

Out of necessity this will be brief – necessity, as all of my time is committed to taking care of Joe - which is far more work than I had anticipated.

Yesterday we brought him home and I have quickly recognized that even with all the help we have here most of the burden (physically) and all of the burden (emotionally) falls upon my shoulders on a daily basis.

But, Joe is home and that is the important thing to note.

Thank you for your caring wishes,
Caryn

Chapter Twelve:
Magical Thinking

Now that Joe was home, I had the gift of distance – distance from the hospital and the fears it had held for Joe and me – to reflect upon our lives together.

Not only had Joe's medical situation been distressing, but throughout his hospitalizations in 2016, we had also faced the passing of far too many dear friends and relatives. A cousin's death was followed by that of a dear friend, which was followed by yet another close friend leaving this realm for the next.

And, so it went, throughout the year with one friend and, or cousin, dying and bringing grief and pain to all of us who were now faced with life without the Earthly presence of each person as he left us.

During the darkest times for me, when Joe was at his most critical point, I would envision a scenario in which I, too, had lost my spouse, my best friend, my love.

As Joe had remained in his bed in Danbury Hospital each evening, I drove home alone, visualizing entering our empty house. It would be lonely, quiet and not at all like home should feel.

I knew I could come in, crank up my music and bop around the house singing to my favorite country songs. In this manner, I might add a bit of life to the loneliness, but doing so would not penetrate the deep silence that pervaded the atmosphere. It was not a peaceful silence but one that was deeply painful. Joe was not home.

Yet, I knew that he would be returning one day. I felt deep within that the combination of his strength, coupled with the skilled medical care he was receiving, would bring him back to our house in the not too distant future.

This was not the case for my cousin and friends who had lost their spouses. Their husbands had passed from this realm to the next and they were learning to live a new normal.

What if it had been my turn to learn that same new normal?

I so did not want this to happen; yet my mind often went to a dark place — one where my thinking could create a reality.

The pain and shame of my thoughts were too deep for me to admit to anyone else, and, so, I kept it all within. Until, finally, one day while sitting with a dear friend who is a psychotherapist, I could no longer hold in the terror within me.

"Normal and natural," she gently declared. We often have anxieties that seep into our psyches unbidden. And in this case, mine were not unusual for a caregiver in my situation. As for believing in the possibility that my wayward thoughts would turn to reality:

"That," she told me, "is magical thinking."

It is magical thinking that makes us assume clicking our fingers will keep the elephants away. It is also magical thinking when we dream of something and believe it will come true.

The Universe just doesn't work that way.

It's true that since I have been clicking my fingers I have had no elephants surrounding my house. But not because of the magical thinking. And, that is what I have come to understand as I contemplated life without Joe.

It is normal and natural, as my friend said, to harbor such dark thoughts in times of great emotional stress such as I was going through with Joe and the loss of my friends.

It is also normal and natural to consider those thoughts being powerful enough to bring about a reality.

And, I believe, it is normal and natural to feel great guilt in believing your dark reflections will come to fruition.

But, in the end, it is only magical thinking. And magical thinking is just that; magical, unfounded and just not going to happen. We are – none of us – so powerful as to change the course of our lives or others with a mere electric impulse arising in our distressed brains.

Magical thinking can bring us to a place of great pain, until we understand that its powers are nonexistent. When I finally came to that realization, I was able to relax, cease feeling guilty and learn to take each day as it came – without the need to cross emotional bridges that I had not yet come to.

All too often I found myself mired in such thinking. I tried to consider how fortunate I am — and would remain — should Joe remain hospitalized for a much longer duration of time than we assumed. Or, if he didn't come home at all.

I have my kids and grandchildren, all of whom are bright and caring and would carry me through the emotional turmoil of an extended solitude.

And I have folks in the field — financial advisors, handymen (and women), and maintenance people who would all aid me in keeping the home front secure and up to date.

I'd be just fine, I recognized. All my needs would be covered.

Well, almost all.

As I crawled into bed one evening, ready to start reading a new book, it dawned on me that I always counted on Joe to recommend my next read. He knows just what authors I enjoy, who has released a new book and has it at the ready for me either in his library or lined up on Kindle.

With whom would I wake up and read the newspapers, commenting on the local gossip and information? Who'd keep me from eating the bagel that looked so luscious yet would make my stomach do painful flips for days after its ingestion? And, who would help me remember to take my Wednesday morning pill to keep my aging bones from becoming too frail?

These are all part of the not-so-little things that keep a loving marriage together. The not-so-little things that strengthen a relationship and help forge a true friendship among partners.

That's what had been missing those many weeks that Joe was hospitalized. The bills were being paid and the house was taken care of. I could sing to my heart's content as I roamed the empty rooms. My friends and family were at the ready should I need to talk or grab a cup of coffee (Starbucks's venti coconut milk cappuccino, please) but I needed more.

I needed Joe. And all the not-so-little things that we shared, like Joe groaning at my country singing and ordering the new Daniel Silva book for me as my next read.

Magical thinking will now take me to places that I want to go – it may not work, but it's a heck of a lot better than letting it bring me to the distressing thoughts that had cluttered my mind when Joe was in the hospital.

Chapter Thirteen:
Being Home

~November, December~

November 2015

It was the finale of the bike ride and I was in St. Augustine, FL on November 16, 2015. The other wives and I had sat together over coffee and talked while we were waiting for the group to arrive at the monument downtown. From there we'd all continue on to the beach for the cyclists to dip their rear wheels in the water to signify the end of a cross-country trek.

What Joe didn't know as he and I celebrated the successful finale of what turned out to be a ridiculously tortuous route, is that the women with whom I had been chatting that morning had all affirmed that we really would rather the guys not go on so long a ride again – at least not for several years. It's so hard to be home without them.

Be careful what you wish for, for it might just come true. I recognized the truth of that the following year.

November 2, 2016, 2:54PM

Dear caring friends and family,

Slow progress and now, after 10 days home, we are getting into a routine and it is not quite so hard. Joe has wonderful therapists and we have an amazing live-in aide here with us. But even with all that, it still takes two of us to help Joe during the day.

I am slowly trying to get back to some life other than this and asked my personal trainer to come next week.

And, I am going to get my hair cut tomorrow during the time that Joe might be napping.

Your cards are all up on the fireplace – I have been able to get them anchored by the bricks, your plants and balloons and flowers are all around the house.

They are all so special. As are you!

Sending you much love,
Caryn

****

November 8, 5:45PM

The feeding tube has been removed!!!!!

Caryn

****

November 13, 2016, 9:32PM

Hi all,

Joe was recovering nicely and even starting to walk a little with help and a walker, but he ended up in the hospital again in the middle of the night last night with high fevers.

He has a urinary tract infection and a kidney infection; he is prone to both because of his suppressed immune system.

I have been in touch with his oncologist who was able to calm me down when I was very concerned that Joe had not had his cancer med today. The doctors in the hospital were wary to give it to him because of his fever, but I was in touch with his oncologist who intends to make sure he gets it tomorrow morning.

Today he was extremely lethargic, slept most of the day, hasn't eaten in two days, and appeared - to me - to be showing signs of another stroke. The medical folks tell me that his behavior is not unusual for someone with a urinary tract infection. I pray they are right and that tomorrow morning when I go back to the hospital he will be better, brighter, with more energy.

I slept there last night but tonight have come home to get a good night's sleep and will get back there early tomorrow morning.

Sending you love, Caryn

****

November 18, 2016, 8:36PM

We made it up to Boston yesterday, so Joe could see his oncologist and neuro-oncologist here and have the usual MRI and other tests done.

I have been so scared to come up – mostly because this was the first time I drove him anywhere by myself and even getting him into the car is a big deal. Transferring him from his wheelchair to his walker to the car is really, really, really hard and I've always had someone helping me do it.

But we did well together – I guess it shows what a good pair we are – and his doctor visits yesterday went well.

Big relief.

We're now at the hotel down the block from the hospital and tomorrow morning will leave Boston and come back home.

Our next big adventure will be getting to a UConn women's basketball game again – we hope to go on Dec. 19th and Joe or I will contact the folks in charge and arrange for handicap seating.

****

Nov 19, 2016, 8:36AM

Our aide – who has been with us 24/7 is taking off from Tues night to Sat morning for her Thanksgiving holiday and we told her that when she comes back we will have her come 9-5:00.

The Sara 3000 – the ridiculously heavy and cumbersome machine that helped us transfer Joe from bed to wheelchair went bye bye yesterday.

Little by little we are finding a bit of normal in our lives

I reached out to all my contacts and am going to start doing workshops again.

And, am gearing up for Thanksgiving. I am determined to do the holiday here and have everyone come. Joe's siblings and our niece and her husband and their fantabulous kids will all be with us. But they all know – and they insist – on doing most of the cooking and preparing.

It will be a gorgeous day!

Much love,
Caryn

****

November 26, 2016, 7:46AM

Dear caring friends and family,

We had a wonderful holiday – the last of the company (Joe's sister and her hubby) from Chicago – left today.

It was not much work, for everyone pitched in while I was able to take care of Joe, but the tumult was a bit much.

However, we wouldn't have traded it for anything – it was miraculous to spend Thanksgiving together.

I hope your Thanksgiving was just as joyous.

Sending so much love,
Caryn

December 2015

December is, of course, a particularly joyous month and that held true in 2015 with the celebration of Joe's 67th birthday on December 6th, followed by Chanukah, and Christmas, time with the kids and grandkids, and waiting for the first snowflakes to fall. After all, what are grandkids for if not to make snowmen and snow forts and to go sledding with?

However, when those first flakes fell the next year, the best we could do was watch from inside house and enjoy their beauty. There would be no playing in the white stuff that year.

December 6, 2016, 3:45PM

Thank you all, our dear friends ...

...for the warm birthday wishes you have sent to Joe via calls and emails and cards. Please forgive this group email but there is no way I can contact you each individually and I don't want your caring to go unrecognized.

I had purchased a small birthday cake and very colorful cap that proclaims, "It's my day" and had them ready at the kitchen table for him this morning.

When our aide and I wheeled him into the kitchen he was so pleased – so much so that he grabbed the hat and put it right on his head. This is not something that Joe would have done in the past so it was fun to see.

His celebration continued with his home-care physical therapist and occupational therapist coming – they have been fantastic! He's improving by leaps and bounds and we love showing off each time they come and they see the improvement that has taken place.

It's not as hard to get him into his wheelchair anymore – we are learning to transfer nicely as he's getting stronger and beginning to use the walker.

A few months ago, I wasn't sure we'd be able to celebrate his birthday.

This is a beautiful and celebratory day.

Sending you all our love, Caryn

****

December 11, 2016, 1:45PM

I have so got to share this - Joe's friend just came and picked him up to take him out to lunch.

As I was getting ready to help Joe down the ramp from the house into the garage, he said to me that he was going to walk down on his own without any help.

I yelled that he cannot do that and told his friend to be ready to pick him up when he falls – I was sooooooo angry at Joe.

And then I watched him walk down the ramp on his own.

Wow – have I got to learn to let go and let him dare to try stuff on his own!

Sending love to all,
Caryn

****

December 15, 2016, 5:50PM

Today Joe told me that when he had been in Brigham and Women's Hospital his one dream – and hope – was to go to Anna Maria Island on the west coast of Florida. All he wanted to do was walk in the sand.

SO......

I immediately started checking out the possibility and called the Beach Cottages where we had stayed in the past. And, booked a trip for February.

Don't know how we'll pull it off, but if that's where Joe wants to go, we will figure it out.

Love to all,
Caryn

December 23, 2016, 10:45AM

Dear family and friends,

Yesterday we went to the urologist who removed Joe's catheter – he is now totally unplugged!

Tomorrow we'll celebrate the last night of Chanukah with the CT kids and grandkids as they'll come to the house for dinner with us.

The boys loved to visit and hide under "Boopah's" ramps.

We're looking forward to a very quiet Christmas day and, like every year, hoping we wake up to snow.

Hugs to all,
Caryn

****

December 28, 2016, 9:56AM

We came up to the Vermont house yesterday – lots of tears as we walked in the door for the first time in almost a year.

The car was jam packed with his special needs equipment – wheelchair, walker, shower chair and I was kind of exhausted after packing and unpacking. But the thrill of being here sure made it worthwhile.

The kids are coming up tomorrow and they'll ski during the days. I will stay home with Joe, but I think he'd be okay on his own here in the house – I'm just not quite ready to leave him.

We had told our aide that she has been fabulous (she has) but we no longer need her help in the house and that when we come back from VT she doesn't have to come to the house any more.

We will, however, invite her to dinner one day soon to thank her.

Love to all, Caryn

Chapter Fourteen:
Much to be Thankful For

Sitting together at our Thanksgiving table and looking at the family members who had travelled great distances to be with us, Joe and I were once again reminded of all for which we have to be thankful.

It is, at times, difficult to cull the good from the pain, but if one looks deeply enough the positives can be found.

Joe is forever my guide in this respect.

In May, when he had the first of his stroke-like episodes due to the leukemia cells that were circulating throughout his body, his speech became labored, but his language skills remained strong and he was thankful for the strength of communication he had retained.

Then in June the second stroke attacked, and he lost his ability to pull words from his mind when wanting to communicate. This was a classic example of expressive aphasia and is a not-uncommon effect of neurological impairment. Yet Joe, true to his optimistic approach to life, was often heard telling friends how fortunate he was that his physical abilities had not been impaired.

In a phone conversation with a friend I actually heard him say, "Fine, I'm really fine."

"Fine?" I yelled. "You have cancer and have suffered debilitating strokes and you are fine???"

He just grinned. Yes, in Joe's mind, he was fine.

Ah, but in August, the leukemia cells ran amok through his central nervous system, rendering him unable to use his right hand or move his legs, and he lost his ability to swallow and speak. Joe was now living in the world he had always feared. The physical abilities he had been so fortunate to retain had left him.

Yet, he considered himself fortunate to eventually leave the hospital, enter rehab and finally come home.

I've often marveled at the "lesser" animals (although there is nothing at all "lesser" about them) that inhabit our world. They appear to take that which is thrown at them, accept it, and move on.

It is only we human animals who have a difficult time with transitions. We fuss and fight change when it comes our way, and all too often find fault with the new without working towards integrating it into our lives. This attitude makes finding thankfulness difficult – sometimes impossible.

We can find ourselves living in a world of grief, hate and disappointment.

Or we can heed the words that had been hanging on a hand-painted plaque outside the rehabilitation gym at Spaulding Hospital:

You get bitter or you get better:
It's that simple. Take what has been dealt
to you, and allow it to make you a stronger
person, or allow it to tear you down.
The choice is yours. Choose wisely.

So, sitting at our Thanksgiving table, knowing that Joe was next to me and partaking of the celebration brought a feeling of gratitude to my heart that was almost overwhelming.

And, Joe being the quintessential optimist, said it all in his toast to our guests when he thanked them for all they had done to support him, and for coming great distances to celebrate the holiday – and life itself – that day.

We do, indeed, have much for which to be thankful.

Biker Joe celebrates the conclusion of his 3,055-mile journey from San Diego, CA to St Augustine, FL, November 16, 2015

A reflective moment between CJ and Joe prior to his discharge from Spaulding Rehabilitation Hospital, Boston, MA July 14, 2016

We had much to celebrate on Joe's birthday December 6, 2016

Getting back to a University of CT women's basketball game on December 19, 2016

*Joe's dream when in Brigham and Women's Hospital was to make it
out of there and feel the sand under his feet on Anna Maria Island, FL.
We made that happen on February 4, 2017*

PART THREE:

A New Year, A New Beginning

Chapter Fifteen:
My Learning Curve

We arrived back in Connecticut from our Vermont house and the holiday week ready to begin a new year, filled with hope and encouraged with Joe's progress.

Yet, there was still so much to accomplish in helping Joe continue to heal, and in helping me, as well – for I had still not learned all of the lessons that were to be taught to me as I continued to be Joe's caregiver, possibly for a very long time.

Naiveté had most certainly taken hold of me at the end of that past year. Especially in the last few days of December.

The idea of New Year's Eve and the promise of 2017 appearing as we blew our party horns, lighted the flares and watched the ball drop in Times Square filled me with great hope; hope that when I awoke on January 1st all that was wrong in the world would have disappeared.

No one would be in pain; all would be peaceful. Did I really believe that friends who had passed would suddenly rematerialize and Joe would have returned to full health and strength?

I awoke New Year's morning with a very heavy heart.

Joe was much better, but he still had a long way to go before regaining all that the strokes of the past year had taken from him.

A New Year's Eve celebration in Istanbul was marred by yet another terrorist attack.

I didn't mysteriously lose the six pounds I had been determined to lose by the New Year.

I realized there is no magic fix. The line of demarcation between one year and another is thin; separated by a fleeting second on the clock, clearly not long enough to repair all the pain of the last year.

As that morning had shown me, the ticking of a clock doesn't make our lives different. It is our attitude that does. That's what New Year's resolutions are all about.

Our resolutions are only as powerful as the ways in which we tackle them. Sitting back and wishing things were different/better/happier/ more peaceful doesn't cut it. Digging in and being active participants in creating the changes we aspire to in our lives and our world is the way to make our declarations move from vision to reality.

Can I magically make Joe all better? Of course not. But continuing to cheer him on as he makes forward strides in his recovery will go a long way towards helping us both.

And, I remain at the ready to help and comfort friends and family members who are still hurting from their past heartaches.

No, the forward movement of the clock's second hand did not make a change in our lives.

But we can.

As we entered January 2017, I was so very weary. Thesaurus.com will tell you the synonyms for that adjective are tired, worn out, exhausted, fatigued, sapped, burnt-out, spent, drained.

And, I felt them all.

But by mid-January, "weary" turned into something much more. I was also angry — not at Joe, but at all that I had on my plate.

Assuming that by this time Joe would be more independent (which he was) and I'd be able to get back to life as normal, I'd gone ahead and rescheduled all the speaking engagements and workshops that I'd contracted for in the past.

Add to this, long-overdue-lunch dates with friends, piles of paperwork on my desk, traveling to see the kids, taking care of the house, even keeping up with my exercising routines, well, it was all too much.

Getting back to "normal" wasn't as easy as I thought it would be, for while Joe was now pretty independent in the house, he still needed a driver to get him to his many doctor and physical therapy appointments. That would, of course, be me—his personal chauffeur.

Any of our many friends would be pleased to jump in and help out with driving and other tasks, but Joe is my husband and I am his caregiver, and all of these jobs should fall on my shoulders. Right?

No. Not right.

I came to that realization one Sunday afternoon when suddenly our calm and peaceful home was invaded by a screaming banshee. She was out of control, running around the house, yelling, banging things and slamming doors.

This dreadful monster that had found her way into our house was, quite to my surprise, looking quite a bit like me—same face, but the eyes were wild. Same voice box, yet the sounds emanating from within were shrill and hitting high notes that on my best singing days I'd never be able to reach. Sad to admit, it was, of course, me.

Where did she come from? She came from 10 months of being caretaker and not letting go, even though it was now time to do so.

She came from not recognizing that I simply cannot accomplish everything—though I tried darn hard to convince myself I could.

I wanted to do it all—continue to help Joe, and begin living again as I'd done before Joe's strokes last year. And it just wasn't possible. That screaming banshee taught me the truth of that.

When I'd finally worn myself out and collapsed into a kitchen chair next to Joe, I'd come to my senses enough to recognize I needed help. I needed Joe's help. I needed help from a saner me. And, I needed help from a professional in the field.

This time I didn't balk at the idea, but went directly to the phone and contacted a local psychologist with whom I'd met in the past.

Three days later, with Joe in tow, I went for my session. The time spent was good, clarifying and uplifting. Both Joe and I learned something about each other that had not formerly come to light and gave us another building block with which to continue strengthening the foundation of our new normal.

Joe shared with us that he had not fully appreciated family and friends visiting, sending cards, and caring emails. He just hadn't recognized the depth of their concern. At some point, he knew he should have realized he was sicker than he thought since his sister often flew in from Chicago, his brother and our kids were there all the time. He simply didn't connect the dots.

And, I let him know how the anxiety and stress of the past eight months had taken its toll on me; how I had tried to hide my emotions from him and that was, indeed, a very difficult thing to do.

It was time for us to begin to understand each other and how we had faced this critical time in our lives. And to discuss the future; our hopes for each other and how we could be more open in our emotional lives.

Most importantly, we discussed the distinction between me being vigilant and hysterical. It is a very fine line, indeed. And, I could finally share with him my erratic behavior on a recent morning when he had chosen to sleep late:

At 8:00 a.m. Joe, who was usually patiently waiting for me to awaken in the mornings, remained comfortably snoozing. Nice. I was able to roll out of bed, shuffle into the shower and dress before helping him through his daily rituals. There was a freeing feeling in spending time on my own – albeit I did not crank up the radio to full volume as I sang under the running water.

He was still sleeping at 8:45 so I toddled off into the kitchen to begin grinding and brewing my coffee. Having inadvertently left our bedroom door open, I was sure Joe would waken to the sound of the coffee grinder — certainly not the way I wanted him to greet the day.

I entered the bedroom, ready to apologize for startling him with the racket from the kitchen. but sleeping beauty was snoring away. How strange. But good that he was enjoying a deep sleep.

When, by 10:00 a.m. Joe, still slumbered away my level of anxiety began to rise. My mind raced to anxious places: *This is not normal. There must be something dreadfully wrong with my man. Perhaps a urinary tract infection. Or a raging case of anemia. Maybe his blood sugar level has dropped to a dangerously low number. Whatever is going on, there is definitely something happening. And, it is disconcerting.*

I texted our visiting nurse. She echoed my concern and suggested I call Joe's oncologist immediately.

Within fifteen minutes, I woke up Joe and got him dressed, brought him into the kitchen for breakfast and informed him that he had half an hour to eat before I tossed him in the car for a ride to see the oncologist's nurse practitioner.

By noon, Joe had endured multiple blood tests, questioning and a physical exam. "He is fine," we are told, "just sleepy." Nothing more ominous than that. He was probably sleepy because he had spent a restless time tossing in bed the night before. We were soon on our way home.

Everything we had been told begs the question: was I being vigilant? Or, did I overreact? Was I being hysterical?

After living through that past year with Joe and his hospitalizations, I often reflect upon the signs that had been occurring, waiting for me to pick up on them before the cancer cells had done their damage. I had missed them all.

Why didn't I realize that his slurred speech was announcing the stroke occurring in his brain? How did I miss the signs of the urinary tract infection (UTI) that had become so insidious that it landed him in the hospital?

Thinking back to that infection, I remember the panic I felt as I saw signs of another stroke, only to be assured by the medical staff that a UTI often produces the same symptoms.

I didn't believe them and pushed for more vigilance from the staff lest Joe be in danger.

They were right in the assessment. I had overreacted. I had been hysterical. But the medical staff had not lived through Joe's strokes with me. They had not watched him go from strong cyclist to the man whose right hand began to weaken, to the patient whose body had been ravaged by massive central nervous system damage.

Of course, they were calm. Of course, I was nervous.

I had been vigilant then because that is what was needed from me then and still is now. It is imperative that I stay alert to changes in Joe's physical condition and behaviors. Yet I must do so in a sensible manner, one that allows for being watchful but precludes panic.

I suspect time and experience will continue to teach me how to balance these two emotions.

Until then, I hope Joe continues to bear with me, recognizes that I'm doing the best I can for him — the man that I love so dearly. I hope he is grateful for my vigilance. And, forgives me for my hysteria.

That meeting with the clinical psychologist had been so very vital to our healing. Just as we need help to deal with the physical demands of caring for our loved ones, we need psychological support to cope with the emotional demands that are also being heaped upon us.

No one is so strong that they are immune to the inner turmoil inherent in being caregiver-in-chief. We all want to do our very best for those under our care, but we also harbor dreams of going back to our "normal" lives — the lives we lived before the illness or physical disability of the person we love became the primary focus of our attention.

We need our own set of skills to navigate these foreign waters and, no matter how much we think we know about working through choppy seas, trust me – we do not know it all. No one does.

And, we especially don't know it all when whatever knowledge we have is overshadowed by our personal apprehension, anxiety and fears.

To begin, I acknowledged that I had to set priorities for myself.

At the top of that list was Joe and continuing to help him. But helping him doesn't necessitate being there every single minute of the day. I realized I could help just as well by lining up friends who would take him to his appointments when they became too numerous for me to keep up with or, if one such appointment conflicted with a workshop that I had promised to facilitate.

Next came those workshops and speaking engagements. They mean so very much to me, fill me with a sense of purpose different from that of being wife and mother. I love the kids with whom I work and don't want to have to give that up.

I love my friends, but realized that setting aside blocks of time I did not have — to sit at lunch with them — created stress which is, of course, not at all conducive to fun and relaxation. So, while my friends themselves did not diminish in importance in my life, for now, carving out time for lunch with them did pop down to third on the rung in my ladder of priorities.

What I also had to learn was letting go and giving Joe space to grow and regain his self-confidence. One of my first lessons came mid-January when he donned his grey herringbone suit, white dress shirt and pewter tie with the deep blue dots in preparation for a retirement party we had been invited to. It was our first foray into the world of social interaction and quite an exhilarating event for us. We were going to be driving to a destination other than our doctors' offices and were going to have conversations that did not revolve around hospitals, diagnoses or surgeries.

For this momentous event, Joe was going to look his best and spiffiest self.

I did not realize he intended to also wear his black dress shoes. The outfit would not be complete, Joe insisted, if he had sneakers sticking out from the bottom of his slacks.

If you are a woman you will relate to the next chapter in this tale, the part that describes the pushing, tugging, swearing and exasperation that comes with stuffing one's feet into lovely but oh, so tight, shoes.

"You Cannot Do This!" I yelled, as every muscle in my body spasmed while forcing the shoes on to his inflamed feet. "You will be in great pain! Your feet will swell even more! You will be miserable!" I grunted, once they were firmly affixed to his feet.

Knowing that I was going to hear Joe complain unendingly during the evening about his aching feet, I secretly stuffed a pair of his slippers into my handbag.

They never left my bag, for my dapper man glowed that evening – every bit of him looking sharp and remaining pain-free throughout the event.

My battle cry of "You cannot do this!" was turned into a contrite, "Oops, yes you can!"

That battle cry was turned upside down again several evenings later when his friend, John, came to pick Joe up and drive him to dinner.

After putting on his winter jacket, Joe eagerly waiting at the side door for his ride to arrive and, when John appeared, Joe decided I did not have to push him in the wheelchair down the very steep ramp out of our house.

He was going to use the walker and descend the ramp on his own.

Now, you need to know that it was only two days ago that he declared he would ambulate from our bedroom to the kitchen — relying on another ramp – longer, but not as steep as the one that exits the house. Holding both my breath and the wheelchair as I walked behind him, I watched as this man with his 'never give up' attitude, succeeded in his venture, arriving safely at the kitchen table.

But the ramp from the house? Never. It was far too steep to be safe. He was absolutely not ready to undertake such an ambitious task.

As Joe began his descent, I yelled for John to be ready to catch him. Surely this was going to end up in some cataclysmic consequence. I railed that I would not take him to the emergency room and most certainly would not visit him in the hospital when he stumbled and tumbled his way down the ramp.

"You cannot do this!" I cried.

And, when he arrived safely at the bottom of the ramp, once again I had to concede, "Oops, yes you can."

There is no limit to what one can achieve when the body and mind are strong. The only thing that holds us back is attitude; the attitude not only of our skeptical selves but that of those around us. I understand that so very well now. And, I vow to never allow my negativity keep Joe from achieving all that he can. Caution is one thing. Discouragement is quite another.

Joe continued his forward strides – literally and figuratively – until, mid-January, the ramps inside the house were removed and he was able to navigate the four steps from family room to kitchen on his own. I do believe the only one upset about the removal of the ramps was our youngest grandson who had enjoyed exciting times "hiding" under them.

So, now I know that my battle cry of "You cannot do this!" must be amended to not, "Oops, yes you can" but to the much more positive, "Of course you can!" You're Joe!

Chapter Sixteen:
A (Slightly) Different Joe

Have you ever gone to a high school reunion? You know, the ones where you work for months beforehand to lose 35 pounds, go to the best plastic surgeon for your neck lift and wrinkle fix, and shop at boutiques you can't afford to purchase the perfect outfit to show off your new figure.

You work so very hard, determined to look your best to earn your former classmate's adoration.

I've never done that. Gone to a reunion, that is. Until today.

Today, Joe and I drove back to Danbury Hospital to sign an insurance form that will allow him to continue receiving his chemo medication. The gal we needed to work with was right at her desk and, so, the task was completed quickly and efficiently.

Looking at my watch, I saw that it was 2:40 p.m. – just 20 minutes before change of shift on the hospital floors. It was a perfect time for our long overdue "reunion" with all the folks who had worked so hard to bring Joe back to his now healthy and healing self.

Joe has worked diligently since he left the hospital three months ago. He has not been out shopping for the perfect clothing, not getting a face-lift or Botox injections. Rather, he has been re-learning to speak clearly, swallow and walk.

As he'd only come with a cane that day in February, rather than his walker, I deemed him in perfect shape to show off his recovered self and thank the staff who had shared their love and skills with us, both during those many weeks spent on their units, first oncology, then rehabilitation.

Joe certainly looked forward to seeing the folks on the rehab floor. He had come out of his haze by the time he'd been transferred there last

October and remembered them all with great fondness. He was eager to show everyone how far he'd come.

And, they were thrilled to see him. I suspect that after patients leave the hospital setting, many don't come back again for a reunion of their own. That would leave the staff wondering how their former charges are doing after their release from the hospital's care.

But there was Joe, securely walking up to the nurses' station with a huge smile on his face. And there I was, grinning from ear to ear, ready to show off my strong and determined husband.

It was most certainly a reunion of monumental proportions with the folks on the rehab unit sharing loving hugs with Joe and me. "We made their day," was the mantra from them all. And, it felt so very good.

The next stop was the oncology floor. Joe was reluctant to go. He didn't remember anyone, he claimed, so why would they remember him? Would they really care? He doubted the necessity of schlepping all the way to that unit.

But, I was insistent. So, we went. And, wow, was that a worthwhile journey.

We entered the area, and before we made it up to the nursing station, nurses and aides and doctors — and love — surrounded Joe and me. So much love.

No, Joe did not remember any of them and that was understandable considering the condition he was in when he'd been there. But, I remembered everyone. I remembered their compassion, the sharing of their expertise, the tenderness they showed in caring for Joe, their kindness in comforting me when I broke down and cried. And, they remembered him.

They came, seemingly, out of the woodwork – jogging out of the back rooms to see the star of the day and marvel at his physical strength and health.

That most certainly was a reunion day I shall never forget. As I reflect upon all that has transpired over the past eight months, I am truly amazed at what Joe had endured.

And, how much he had changed. Not only from the severely ill man who had been lying in a hospital bed just six months earlier, but the man who I had known as Joe, even before his illness had struck.

Joe is softer now. While he has always been a caring and tender person, the post-stroke Joe is even more so.

As revealed by his new friend, Buddy.

Joe and I have lovingly cared for several four-legged children. The last two were huge Old English Sheepdogs named Ditto and Daniece.

Ditto was the brother of Daniece's mother, thus his niece. Hence her name, Daniece.

We loved them fiercely and when they died there was a void in our lives. Yet, we were reluctant to fill that vacancy. The loss was too painful to undergo again with another dog. And, because we travel often, we were often worried about their care.

I, however, have not yet ceased hounding (pun intended) Joe for another pooch companion, but he has been (almost) convincing in his resolve to not adopt another.

So, I content myself with my numerous stuffed animals and the recognition that Joe is absolutely correct. When it is cold in the winter, raining in the spring, ghastly hot in mid-summer, I know I would not like to be walking a dog in the elements.

And, when we travel it is, I admit, nice to not worry about finding a pet sitter. We can pick up and go whenever we want without having to plan for a dog's care.

Recently, while spending some time in our vacation home in Vermont, our daughter came for a visit and she and I went shopping at some of the more fun boutiques in a neighboring town.

During that jaunt, she found, purchased and approached me with the most adorable little bear doll. Only a foot tall, dressed in matching winter hat and jacket, long nose thrust forward helping to create a doleful expression, he grabbed at my heart. And, I excitedly brought him back to the house to sit at the kitchen table. I assumed that is where he'd remain to greet us every time we went back up to Vermont.

But, two days later, after packing the car for our trip back home, with Joe waiting for me in the passenger seat, I peeked into the kitchen and saw my little bear sitting at the table. He definitely wanted to come back to Connecticut with us. There was no doubt. And, so, I grabbed him, and tossed him in Joe's lap as I got into the car.

"Please take care of the bear on the ride home. He really wants to come with us."

I half expected a shrug, a reluctant acceptance, and nothing more.

What I did not expect was to glance at Joe from time to time and see him smiling tenderly at the bear. There was definitely a bond forming.

Once home, I positioned him (the bear, not Joe) in the fruit bowl on the kitchen counter and, during dinner later that evening, caught Joe gazing at the bear, pointing to him, smiling and acknowledging his presence in our home.

Something was beginning to happen here. And, it was something I had not expected, for, while Joe is a gentle and compassionate man, he had never reacted to an inanimate object like that before, certainly not a stuffed animal.

Eventually, the bear found its way into the basket on Joe's walker and Joe, now true to form, would greet it (the bear, not the walker) with a smile and pat on its head.

One day I'd removed the bear from Joe's walker basket as it was near the shower while Joe was washing and I didn't want to have it get wet. This was disturbing to Joe for, when he got out of the shower, he immediately noticed his newfound pal missing and asked where his buddy was.

Ah, so now it had a name: Buddy.

Buddy has since been moved to our bed, as Joe no longer needs the walker. And, Buddy was even devious enough to find his way into our luggage when we went to Anna Maria Island last month. He appeared under the covers and, when Joe discovered him, his pleasure was unmistakable.

All week long, Buddy kept us company — although we did not allow him to come with us to the beach. But, being the patient guy he is, he waited in the cottage for our return and Joe's hearty, "Hey Buddy. How you doing?"

Here's the thing, this caught me totally off-guard. I'd never had one of my stuffed animals hijacked before. Never has Joe wanted to adopt any of the group — no matter how cute and cuddly they were.

But, there is something in Buddy that speaks to Joe. And there is a new — or perhaps enhanced, quality in Joe that is listening to whatever it is Buddy is saying to him.

I am so very thankful to Buddy for allowing my strong, self-assured husband to allow a softer side to surface so openly.

I'm just sitting back, taking it all in, and marveling at Joe and Buddy and what their friendship has brought them both.

That softer side of Joe popped out again more recently in regard to a family of geese that live on our property.

Momma and poppa goose come to visit every spring. Mom builds a nest, on an island in our little pond, for her eggs and waits patiently for the goslings to hatch, while dad patrols the rest of the grounds making sure all is safe. Within a month, we awaken one morning to the sight of a brand-new family parading around the yard. Momma at the front, six or seven kids behind her and dad pulling up the rear.

This year, however, after a mere week, they all disappeared. Joe was distressed, looking out for them every morning, having me help him walk down to the pond in the afternoon. And, when they suddenly reappeared several weeks later his relief was unmistakable.

I will never say that Joe has become childlike – that would be unfair – but there is an innocent quality that has popped out in his demeanor and it is totally endearing.

For instance, recently I had been driving us both to visit a friend and Joe was giving me directions (he is amazing at this direction thing while I am totally directionally challenged) but we would almost be on top of a particular street when he'd tell me to make a turn. It is frustrating when he does this and makes driving difficult. And, so, I called him on it when we arrived home. "Don't you realize I cannot make a right hand turn on a second's notice without, perhaps, crashing into the car next to me?" His response came with the most guileless facial expression. "I can't come up with the words quickly enough to tell you in time."

This innocence is part of the new Joe and, I must say, it is endearing and lovely.

But, there are times when he drives me crazy – and mostly those are during dinner.

Joe's taste buds have changed.

Joe loves his burgers – especially the ones at the local fast food joint. These patties of meat are flattened (probably between two bricks), smothered in sauce, flipped onto a roll and served today, just as they'd been served to customers for the past forty-six years.

Me? I'd rather have just the fries, but Joe has long relished (no pun intended) these delicacies. Until recently.

Actually, until recently he has all kinds of burgers, salmon, chicken, meatloaf – all the things that I love to serve us for dinner. They are easy to prepare, and make the main portion of our meals hearty and, if I've done my job well, tasty.

We don't know if his cancer medication is the culprit, or perhaps the damage to his central nervous system, but something has decided to prey on his taste buds and cause them to dislike just about everything he had previously enjoyed.

For his part, the lack of taste for the aforementioned proteins is not as big a deal as his distaste for beer and coffee.

Good for me – I get to drink the entire coffeepot by myself. Beer, on the other hand, does nothing for me.

Joe's new taste bud bias is driving me nuts. Bad enough that it's annoying for him, but, golly, as the one who does the cooking in the house I am beginning to develop a complex. And, anyone watching me trot through the local grocery store would think me in a perennial state of confusion. No, I am not at the beginning throes of dementia. I just wander up and down the aisles trying to come up with an idea for a meal that will suit Joe's new demanding palate.

The other night he suggested I serve roasted chicken, coleslaw and potato salad. Wow. That was a surprise as only the week before he had not been able to tolerate chicken. So off to the food store I went to purchase one of their roasted chickens (natural, no hormones, not too much salt, very tasty and pretty healthy), grabbed some coleslaw and potato salad and started walking away from the deli counter when I noticed that at the hot food section they were offering mashed potatoes – a particular favorite of Joe's. I could not pass them up and, so, returned the potato salad to the shelf and got a huge portion of the freshly made mashed potatoes.

When I arrived home, I excitedly placed our dinner on the table waiting for Joe's words of, something like, "Wow, mashed potatoes, thanks honey!" and I would reply, "You're welcome, I knew you'd love them."

Instead I heard, "Whose idea were the mashed potatoes?" When I proudly responded, "Mine," Joe said, "I don't like them."

"Since when?"

"Since yesterday. I guess I should have told you."

As the kids would text, "OMG!"

One physician's assistant recently suggested having him suck on a lemon prior to digging into his meal. The tartness of the lemon, it seems, reinstates the taste buds and might allow him to enjoy food again.

It did work the one time Joe agreed to try it.

Can someone please explain to me why he won't do it again? He just shrugs his shoulders when I present him with a lemon, or lemon sorbet or even a lemon candy.

As I sit here writing this chapter, I am observing Joe and his breakfast routine. Ah – yet another "eating" predicament, for, while he is totally capable of chewing, swallowing and enjoying his daily English muffin slathered with butter and jelly, he does so in a frustratingly dawdling manner.

There is he, knowing that we must leave for a doctor's appointment in fifteen minutes, and he still insists on following every post and video on Facebook. Ingesting his breakfast is an afterthought - and it drives me crazy, as I need to continually warn him of the time limitation before having to hop in the car and get to the medical office. In this case, Joe is more of a teenager than a child. And, I already lived through that era with our kids. I don't really love doing it again. Well, I sort of love it – it is kind of cute.

After all, it is the new Joe and how could I not love him?

I'm told we are not alone in these dilemmas. Many caregivers have shared similar stories with me. If you are among them, please send me an email and let me know how you have handled these personality transformations. Thanks.

Chapter Seventeen:
Life Redux

Little by little life has taken on a more "normal" look, albeit not quite the same as it was last year, before Joe's illness hit.

Together, we have learned to weather the storms and tackle each new situation with, I am pleased to report, a continuing, positive outlook and much laughter.

When Joe was at Spaulding Rehabilitation Hospital in Boston last July he had visions of going to Anna Maria Island in Florida to relax and walk in the sand.

This simple thought carried with it a world of hope — hope that he would eventually leave the hospital; would once again be "normal" and would be able to enjoy the simple pleasures of life.

Many folks in his position might harbor visions of traveling to the Caribbean or some exotic far-away island. But Joe's wishes were humbler, meandering on the sands of little known Anna Maria Island, a throwback to simpler times. It seemed out of reach at the time but certainly a goal worth working towards.

And, then came his discharge, our return home to Connecticut, a whirlwind of doctors' appointments and physical therapy visits. We were certainly too busy to even think of leaving our home base. By mid-summer, we might have begun booking our flights when the cancer cells struck once again, and attacked his central nervous system.

A trip to Anna Maria was unquestionably out of reach. Recovering and leaving the hospital was even an uncertainty.

Those who know Joe are not surprised that nine weeks after the beginning of his hospitalization, he was discharged. Three months later that trip to the beach was beginning to look like it might be a reality.

So, when he began to discuss it again in January, I started my research and began with a conversation with a friend whose husband had recently suffered a stroke – yet they were able to travel to Florida recently.

"How do you do it?" I asked my friend. "How the heck are you flying to Florida just a year after he had his last stroke?"

My friend's response was direct, "Make it as easy on yourself as possible; garner all the help necessary; take time for adequate planning, and you'll be just fine."

Thus, began a conversation that led me to believe Joe and I would be able to fly down to Anna Maria Island, Florida in February.

It had been more than a year since we'd been able to travel – well, excluding our wild ambulance rides from time to time. And, while I wanted to honor Joe's vision of walking in the sand, I did not want to be delusional in thinking we could make his dream come to fruition.

I went back to the drawing board that held my to-do list of travel plans and started filling in the blanks.

First, I realized that it would be less of a strain on my back and psyche if I didn't have to deal with checking and retrieving luggage at both ends of each flight. Therefore, a week prior to our departure, I schlepped three cardboard boxes of summer clothing to the local UPS store and had them ship it to our hotel. The hotel staff was then contacted and asked to expect the delivery prior to our arrival. No problem there — they were extremely kind (even put the boxes in our room when they arrived).

As for the pesky "carry-on" items I could not do without? Well, they were stuffed into the lightest backpack I owned and were, therefore, easy enough to deal with.

Next on the list was a call to a local limo service to request picking us up at home and delivering us to the airport. In this manner, I avoided having to park my own car and then take a van to the terminal from the parking lot the day of our flight.

I was cranking and on a roll.

Talking about roll, we needed a wheelchair for Joe at the airport to get to the departure gate and yet another waiting at the arrival gate in Tampa. Easy enough. All that required was a call to the airline, which was happy to accommodate us. With all the car rental companies nestled together at the Tampa International Airport, I quickly figured out that with the help of a kind wheelchair pusher we would be able to get to our vehicle.

Coming home was merely a reversal of our steps going.

Was I skeptical about the trip? I most certainly was, for I knew it would take much extra effort to pull it off; sending our luggage ahead of time via UPS, ordering wheelchairs at each airport and having a car service drive us to and from our destinations.

Would Joe be able to push his walker around the rocky areas of the cottages where we'd be staying? And, making his way down to the beach, let alone walking on the sand, would likely be out of the question. Perhaps we would be able to see the ocean from afar and that would have to suffice.

But, Joe is a strong dude. He is strong of spirit and body, so I should not have been surprised when he decided to forgo the walker and only use a cane during our stay at Anna Maria.

And, I should not have been surprised, either, to watch him not only walk to the beach, but also take his long-anticipated steps on the sand, and make his way down to the ocean.

We even got to sit in beach chairs at the edge of the ocean. That, by the way, provided a good laugh not only for us but others who were watching as I tried to pry Joe up and out of the beach chair at the end of the day. He could not get up on his own and I was giggling too hard to be of much help. Fortunately, two very kind women came over to give us a hand or we might still be sitting there now.

Not all dreams are actualized. In Joe's case, this one was. It happened because he believed. And, belief is a powerful thing. Without that we cannot achieve our goals. With a strong belief system, much hard work, Joe's positive attitude, his dream became a reality.

We also believed in the strength of our marriage and love for each other and that has helped immensely as we hit upon small snafus in our day-to-day lives.

For instance, there is the problem of my new back seat driver: Joe – who used to be our chauffeur and now, until very recently, had to deal with me taking over that position.

Recently, we've had some exchanges about this that were less than comfortable. They have led to minor yelling matches (and, please believe me when I say that we are not a couple who yell at each other), and hurt feelings (mostly mine).

"Stay in your lane." "Get over, there's traffic entering the highway!" "You're going too fast/slow/crooked/straight." "I don't trust that bus ahead of you, pass it!" "Why did you pass that bus?" "Why did you let that car into the lane?" And, sprinkled in there might be a few (or more than a few) choice expletives.

We have all been told at one time or another that we need to speak our minds. Harboring negative thoughts often lead to misunderstandings among friends. Holding back when we need to discuss a point can bring about unnecessary confusion, misunderstandings and dissention.

Yet, when a loved one is weakened we want to be the voice of positivity and smile through all our caregiving chores. After all, we most certainly don't want to complain, do we? That would send the wrong message, one that might express, "Well, I am taking care of you but, golly, this is hard stuff and I would rather not be doing this."

I highly doubted that he expresses his anxiety in same manner when his brother or friends drive and, so, despite much trepidation, I called him on it. "This is not nice, and you are making me a more nervous and unstable driver because of your criticism," I told him.

His response was to remind me about his inability to be a relaxed passenger. That's when I suggested his condemnation of my driving ability was more vocal and incessant than it must be when he rides in someone else's car. Joe replied that I was incorrect. He's the same way with everyone.

Now, I am not writing this piece to condemn him, but to bring to light the next chapter in this anecdote.

Two days later, I drove Joe to a local doctor's appointment and noticed that there was no disapproval of my driving ability. Nor was there negativity yesterday as we traveled to yet another meeting.

More recently, as we drove to Vermont, he was also uncharacteristically silent about the way I was handling the car. So, I asked if he was purposely remaining quiet and not chastising me about the way I was getting us from point A to point B in our Subaru lately.

His response was a gentle, "Yes."

I had needed to speak up and let Joe know that his condemnation of my driving was difficult to take and was invading the joy in our relationship. That is the speaking up we must do as caregivers if we want to continue to do our jobs with love, eschewing any possible resentment.

That is also the "speaking up" that our loved ones need to practice, especially when they must submit to having someone do tasks for them that they used to do themselves. Joe did need to speak up at times when my driving was less than sterling. (Shall I admit here that I am not a perfect driver?). It was the manner in which he did it that hurt me.

But, our conversation led to a renewed tolerance of our individual needs and an improvement in our communication skills.

Albeit a different manner of communicating in some instances, for, with Joe's expressive aphasia there are often times when he wants to tell me something, but the words are just not there. That's when we begin a game that resembles a fusion of twenty questions and charades. Someone watching us might think it frustrating. And, it is for Joe, I am sure, but we manage to find the light side of it and are often quite amused as I continue to improve my ability to figure out what he wants to articulate.

Joe is now driving a bit again – short trips to local venues. I must admit that when I am his passenger I often have to hold my tongue lest I sound like he did when I drove.

It is difficult, isn't it, to sit in the passenger seat and not be in charge? And, now it is he who must speak up and tolerate my back-seat commentary.

As with the division of our driving duties, so, too, have Joe and I fallen into a comfortable routine with the segmentation of labor in the house.

While both of us are capable people, we've found our niches within the relationship, with Joe staking out financial advisor, household efficiency engineer, bar-b-que guru and brewer/server of my morning coffee.

I juggle being social engineer, domestic manager, purchaser of the birthday cards that he dutifully signs, executive chef responsible for planning meals, line cook, baker and spender of the money that Joe so carefully balances.

It works, and we love our lives and each other, unequivocally.

Then, several years ago after my last back surgery, Joe had added to his role the title of caregiver when, upon my return home, he became head nurse as I stumbled around the house, unable to take care of myself physically, and, at times, emotionally.

As the saying goes, "he stepped up to the plate." But that was neither unusual nor unexpected. Joe has always established himself as the caregiver in our relationship; he is the strong one, the one who can be counted on to fix problems and keep our lives in order. This, while spectacular in scope, was just one more example of Joe taking care of me.

Last year it became my turn to don the title of caregiver, and I only hoped I could be as capable in fulfilling my new role as Joe had been for me.

I believe I was.

And, he accepted and appreciated my help as I stayed with him in a hospital far from home, conversed with the doctors trying to make sense of their medical jargon, kept friends and family up-to-date on the various details of Joe's condition and progress, made decisions about the best and safest procedures to be carried out, and ran the household from afar — paying bills and organizing household care.

Was it a perk to be able to now care for Joe?

Perhaps. I surprised my kids and myself with my capable, organizational and rational approach. I did not surprise Joe. He assumed me to be a woman of such strength. And, he most certainly appreciated having me take over this custodial role now that it was necessary for me to do so.

But, there was also an unexpected bonus. Our love grew in indefinable ways. We have grown stronger. And, we have discovered a new depth to our relationship that we might have before thought unimaginable.

In his hospital room, Joe and I often sat looking at each other recognizing the truth of what I am saying here. Yet it is something that defies description, even for this woman who lives her life through her spoken and written words.

Simply put, Joe and I love each other with a heightened intensity that perhaps we would not have found if not for his illness.

Like the Yin and Yang — those complimentary forces that make up our lives — we have found through adversity an incredible gift. The past year has brought great stress, but it has also borne great rewards as Joe and I learned to rely on each other in more ways than we could have imagined. We have found a combined inner strength we never knew was there, and our love and admiration for each other is stronger than it has ever been in spite of, and because of, that which we have endured together.

Chapter Eighteen
One Pedal at a Time

I am writing this final chapter while reflecting upon our recent wedding anniversary and that joyous observance with our children and grandchildren.

Sitting at the table after dinner, surrounded by our loving and supportive family offering toasts of celebration, there was much laughter. And, many tears. For not only did we observe our twenty-six years of marriage, we marked an even more notable milestone; the year anniversary of Joe's first stroke and the ensuing hospitalizations, medical turmoil and the subsequent triumph over almost overwhelming odds.

Recalling last year, a profusion of memories filled my mind, each thought battling for primacy, as each took a turn thrusting itself into the limelight, before being shoved into the background by another.

I pictured Joe's inability to speak clearly. This was the first sign of his illness. Yet we went ahead and held our anniversary celebration with our children and grandchildren. We laughed, took photos, and enjoyed the day and each other's company. The merriment was dampened greatly, however, by a relentless whispered concern, "There is something wrong and we are frightened."

Joe had known all along that something was wrong; that he had suffered a stroke, yet he said nothing and greeted our anniversary day as if all was perfect and he hadn't a problem in the world.

It is only recently, when Joe had been interviewed for this book, that I discovered the depth of his knowledge. He recalls the "worst pain in the world" on August 24, 2016, the day his Danbury hospitalization began. He spoke of the "awful" sores in his mouth from the chemo drug the doctors gave him to try and stop the cancer cells from doing further damage to his central nervous system. Joe shared that at one point he was convinced they had moved the hospital so, when he looked outside of his window and saw the white of the buildings in the late afternoon sun, he thought he was seeing snow; he had no idea it was summer. The lines between reality and fiction were terribly blurred – so much so that I finally discovered the reason for him having called me "bitch" that day when I wouldn't allow him to get out of bed. It appears that he was convinced I had been holding him prisoner in that hospital room. Ah, so now I understand. And forgive. I knew at some point it would become clear and the pain of hearing that has now turned to amusement.

Joe says he never had a sense that he was going to die. Good for him. I wish I had been that optimistic.

Once home, he was cognizant of me having to get him lifted from bed to wheelchair, and of the ramps that took over our house. When remembering the special equipment being taken away as he began to regain his motor skills, Joe did contemplate that, "I guess that was miraculous." And grinned as he recalls Dr. Jacobsen calling him a "miracle person."

While recollections of doctors' visits, fact gathering, tests and more tests, hospitalizations and fear flooded my head this past year, I have also learned to take comfort in Joe's new appreciation for life.

He has put life in a new perspective; "Yankees and Red Sox, I don't care anymore. British Open – didn't miss it. Didn't watch a minute of the Tour de France, because life is more important." Is that because of the strokes? "Not sure, but life is now more about family and friends."

I believe strongly that the principal take-away from this past year; the message that comes through loud and clear is Joe's eternally positive attitude, "There was never any fear, no anger, because it just was. These feelings are not because of the stroke, that's who I am…never angry for one second because I'm sixty-eight years old, I've had a wonderful life."

As for me, well, Joe and had I always known we are here for each other in any circumstance life might toss in our paths, but this past year we both discovered that my inner strength, physical stamina and

– may I be blunt – my ability to rise to the occasion and be quite assertive when necessary, was far greater than either of us ever imagined.

Being Joe's caregiver was a job I had never asked for, was completely unprepared for, and was totally uneducated in the skills I'd had to employ. But, we often learn well under fire. I recognized that and undertook this new role with a determination to do my very best for Joe.

I became a medical student, psychologist and physical therapist. I studied information about chronic lymphocytic leukemia and stroke, their paths and treatment, how hospitals and the staff function, and leaned I am a far more capable woman than I knew.

I believe I've done well. I had much help in the form of loving and caring friends, family members and dedicated medical staff.

But it is Joe's fortitude that truly keeps us going. Joe is intent on becoming, once again, the physically strong cyclist he was before the cancer wreaked havoc with his central nervous system last spring. For it took determination to cycle across the country despite the numerous obstacles Mother Nature threw his way.

If you have been on a bike you will understand that a great amount of balance is required, as well. Lose that and you will tumble.

As Joe walks around the house, I study his posture and facial features. Every day he appears more comfortable, more balanced, in all capacities.

Thinking about Joe's accomplishments I have come to recognize their impact on my life, as well.

It was on November 16, 2015, that I had been awaiting Joe's arrival in St. Augustine, Florida, as he and his buddies pedaled their bikes the last few miles of their journey that had begun in San Diego, California two months earlier. And, it was on November 16, 2016, that I was awaiting Joe's arrival in our kitchen as he and his aide pushed his wheelchair the last few feet of their journey that had begun in our bedroom several minutes earlier.

What a difference a year can make.

I was acutely aware of the year anniversary even before I sat at the kitchen table watching Joe get teary-eyed, viewing the videos his cycling pals had posted on Facebook that morning. He was viewing clips from their cycling trip across the country the previous year: a memory that will stay with us both forever.

But, it is Joe's optimistic attitude with which we remember this great achievement of his that will make the difference in our lives going forward. For we can look back through that rear-view mirror and bemoan that which might never be again, or we can revisit the past and be thankful for what we once had.

Joe and I are fortunate for what we have had together. And, we are grateful for what we still have, albeit, not quite the same. But, we are facing this new chapter in our lives with the same determination that took Joe across the country — mile by mile — enjoying the scenery and camaraderie along the way.

So, it is with all things in life. Nothing is stagnant. We all know that. Yet, somehow, when we look back upon our days, we are often tempted to bemoan that which we've lost.

That is why it is often said to not look at life through a rear-view mirror, but to look ahead to the future.

In my estimation, looking ahead to the future requires a glimpse back to the past from time to time. We need to reflect upon, and be thankful for, the gifts we have been given.

And, understand that our futures will build upon the strengths and gifts we have been given.

Don't bemoan the adventures in which you might no longer be able to engage. Instead, be thankful they were once yours to enjoy.

I am facing a time of uncertainty as Joe continues to gain in strength and ability. My future is not as well defined as I once believed it to be. I now know I can take nothing for granted. Not personally, nor globally.

I, too, need to keep my balance. I need to work through the trepidation and remain determined — determined that the future will be all right as long as I remain confident and strong in body and spirit.

We all do.

Joe and I must hold on to the lesson we've learned as he continues to regain his former abilities.

That lesson is we are not alone in this uncertain world and we need to find others who will support us in our aspirations and endeavors. They are there for us as we are there for them.

Let the trepidation that threatens to hold us back from achieving our desires be overshadowed by the knowledge that we all have each other's backs. Remain determined to continue to work together towards our collective and personal goals. And, let's keep our confidence — and our equilibrium intact.

At one of the UConn women's basketball games that we were able to attend back in January, the woman seated behind me glanced at Joe and said to me, with great caring, "It must be so very hard for you."

"Yes," I stated, "yet in many ways not, for whatever Joe and I had to endure was well worth the effort." I was so very proud of his ability to fight and get back to the Joe we all knew prior to the strokes. And, I was proud that I played a part in that healing.

Joe has not yet completely recovered; he has some minor cognitive issues; his speech is still a bit slurred and word retrieval is not quite perfect. But his mind, his intelligence, his sense of humor and love of life have not diminished in the slightest. Friends who had not seen him for a while constantly comment on how good he looks. He does and not only compared to the more diminished Joe he had been last year or even three months ago. Joe looks great, actually – although he doesn't fully understand the reason for the comment. To all of us who know and love him, he looks healthy, he looks happy, he looks, well, like Joe.

While writing this chapter I stopped to ask Joe what he sees when looking in the mirror. His response was, "I don't look so good." When I dug further into that remark he added, "Prior to the strokes, I would look in the mirror and see a 19-year-old. Now I see an old man who is compromised physically." Ah, but then he continued with this beautiful statement, "But when I'm riding my bike I feel 19 again."

As a long-distance biker, Joe had the stamina and fortitude to get through even the most difficult terrain as he rode from Virginia and Oregon in 2009. Three years later he pedaled from the Mexican border to the Canadian border over the Sierra Cascade ridgeline. Then, just a year before his illness struck, he endured the now infamous trip from San Diego to St. Augustine, Florida, including the punishing route through 1,000 miles of Texas heat, floods, fire, hailstorms fire ants and tent-invading raccoons.

That experience, in particular, strengthened my hope and resolve that Joe would be capable of withstanding his medical challenges.

This past year was challenging, frustrating, emotionally and physically exhausting: much like the Texas segment of Joe's last cross-country bike ride. When I had asked him how he did it — how he persevered — his response was, "One pedal at a time."

And, this past June he borrowed a recumbent bike from Vermont Adaptive Ski and Sports and participated, once again, in the Long Trail Century Ride. It took him four hours, but he rode twenty arduous and hilly miles. Joe has since purchased, and has begun to ride, a recumbent of his own. He is even planning on joining Adventure Cycling again next September to ride the distance of Route 66 – from Chicago to Los Angeles.

Texas has become the metaphor for his illness for, as he had pedaled his way through those thousand miles of heat, floods, fire, hail and raccoons so, too, did he - and I - make it through his health challenges.

There is no way to know how far Joe will come in his recovery – much as none of us know the future of our lives and health – but we shall forge ahead on the premise that his progress will continue as we keep learning how to care for each - one treatment at a time, one learning at a time, one step at a time…

…one pedal at a time.

Resources for the Caregiver

Now, after the excitement has calmed down; after Joe is back on his feet again; after I am able to breathe and resume some semblance of normal; I've had the time to poke around the Internet and find people who have information about resources for the caregiver.

When in the midst of our calamity, there was no time to undertake such a search and, so, I relied solely upon the information that was handed to me by caring and knowledgeable people in my life.

This was all invaluable but, in retrospect, I wish I had had the time, energy or foresight to garner even more knowledge.

However, now I do have the ability to undertake such a search and am eager to share with you that which I have since learned about resources for the caregiver.

Know that this is not a complete list by any means, but meant to let you know there is much out there waiting to help you; people and organizations – both local and nation-wide – who are ready to provide assistance in an abundance of ways:

FINANCIAL RESOURCES

*Meals on Wheels
https://www.mealsonwheelsamerica.org
1-888-998-6325

*Social Security benefits
https://www.ssa.gov
1-800-772-1213

*Energy assistance
http://www.acf.hhs.gov

*Medicaid
https://www.medicaid.gov

*Today's Caregiver
https://resources.caregiver.com
954-893-0550

STATE AND COMMUNITY BASED GROUPS
(I cannot list all the states but am sharing these few, knowing that they can help you find a resource in your area.)

*Hospice
https://regionalhospicect.org
203-702-7400

*Palliative Care
https://getpalliativecare.org

*Hospital-centered and professional caregiver support groups
http://portal.ct.gov/search-results/?q=caregiver%20support%20groups
(There is similar organization in just about every large state. I suggest an Internet search for "caregiver support groups near me")

*New York State Office for the Aging
https://aging.ny.gov/Caregivers/Index.cfm
844-697-6321

*Connecticut Community Care
https://ctcommunitycare.org
866.845.2224

NEWSLETTERS AND MAGAZINES

*Caregiving Magazines
https://caregiver.com/magazine
https://www.caregiver.org/newsletters
http://www.providermagazine.com/caregiving
https://www.agingcare.com/info/membership-newsletter
http://www.comfortofhome.com/caregiver-assistance-news

NATIONAL CAREGIVING GROUPS

*AARP Caregiving Resources
 https://www.aarp.org/caregiving/?intcmp=FTR-LINKS-
CRGVNG-CRC- EWHERE

*Rosalynn Carter Institute for Caregiving
 http://www.rosalynncarter.org
 229-928-1234

*Caregiver Action Network
 www.caregiveraction.org

*Family Caregiver Alliance
 https://www.caregiver.org
 1-800-445-8106

SPECIFIC TOPIC SUPPORT GROUPS

*Alzheimer support
http://alz.org/ct/index.asp
1-800-272-3900

*Cancer
 https://www.cancercare.org/support_groups
1-800-813-4673

*Stroke

http://www.strokeassociation.org/STROKEORG/LifeAfterStroke/Life-After- Stroke_UCM_308546_SubHomePage.jsp
 1-888-478-7653

*Brain Trauma
 http://www.biausa.org/brain-injury-family-caregivers.htm
 703-584-8642

*Aphasia
 https://www.aphasia.org/site

*Parkinson's Disease
 https://www.michaeljfox.org/understanding-parkinsons/living-with- pd/topic.php?support-groups&navid=support-groups

*ALS
 www.alsa.org/community/support-groups
 1-800-782-4747

*Spousal Support
 http://http://wellspouse.org
 1-800-838-0879

*Elder Care
 https://www.agingcare.com
 239-594-3222

*MS
 https://www.nationalmssociety.org
 1-800-344-4867

SOCIAL MEDIA

https://www.facebook.com/CaregivingSupport/
https://www.facebook.com/FamilyCaregiverAlliance
https://www.facebook.com/FamilyCaregiverfoundation/

Acknowledgments

My thanks go to so many people; those who cared for Joe during his illness and recovery; and those who cared for me during this challenging time in our lives.

He and I are forever grateful to Dr. Robert Ruxin in Sandy Hook, CT., who was suspicious of Joe's low white blood count found in a routine blood test and suggested he check with a hematologist/oncologist.

We are indebted to Dr. Vincent Rella, the head of oncology at Danbury Hospital, the hematologist/oncologist whose caring and skill ultimately brought Joe back from his perilously dangerous illness. We are thankful, as well, for Joe's two primary doctors at Dana Farber Cancer Institute – oncologist Dr. Eric Jacobsen and neuro-oncologist, Dr. Lakshmi Nayak who were, and still are, active in his continuing care along with Dr. Rella.

Joe found confidence when physical therapist extraordinaire, Jeff McKay, had his hands close to Joe's sides to help him find his balance as he relearned how to walk. This remarkable professional, along with his boss, Paul Badger, have helped us both find our balance as we continue to move forward into our unknown futures.

Not forgotten are the many other doctors, nurses and members of the support staff at Dana-Farber Cancer Institute, Brigham and Women's Hospital, Spaulding Rehabilitation Hospital and Danbury Hospital.

We are grateful, as well, to the nurses, therapists and professional caregivers who arrived at our doorstep when Joe came home.

Please forgive me for not mentioning all of your names, but I suspect you know who you are. I sure hope you do, because we will never forget you.

We all understand the importance of family and friends and never more so than when they gather around at times of difficulty. There is a saying that "Friends are the family you choose." Joe and I sure chose well. As for our siblings, nieces and nephews, aunt, cousins, children and grandchildren – there are no words to adequately thank you for your support. We could not have met this challenge without your love and encouragement.

This book came to be with the guidance of Adria Henderson, who was not only my editor but research assistant, as well.

My gratitude goes to my publisher, Angela Hoy, and all the talented people at Abuzz Press for bringing *One Pedal at a Time* to life.

I've turned to many perceptive folks for their input throughout the writing of this book. You have all been remarkably patient and helpful. Especially you, Joe.

About the Author

CJ Golden author of *Tao of the Defiant Woman* and *Tao-Girls Rule!* is an inspirational force for women and teen girls. Caring for her husband after his strokes, Golden faced her ultimate challenge and discovered she had learned well that which she has preached to others all of these years. Sharing her experiences as Joe's caregiver she reached, and helped, thousands of followers through her daily emails and blogs. Golden has received an education in caregiving beyond her expectations and is eager to help others through the knowledge she has gained.

Made in the USA
Middletown, DE
20 May 2018